Blessed Are the Persecuted

IVO LESBAUPIN

Blessed Are the Persecuted

Christian Life in the Roman Empire,
A.D. 64–313

Translated from the Portuguese by
Robert R. Barr

ORBIS BOOKS
Maryknoll, New York 10545

The Catholic Foreign Mission Society of America (Maryknoll) recruits and trains people for overseas missionary service. Through Orbis Books Maryknoll aims to foster the international dialogue that is essential to mission. The books published, however, reflect the opinions of their authors and are not meant to represent the official position of the society.

Originally published as *A Bem-Aventurança da Perseguição*, © 1975 Editora Voces, Rua Frei Luís, 100, 25600 Petrópolis, RJ, Brazil and *La Bienaventuranza de la Persecucion*, © 1983 Asociación Ediciones La Aurora, Buenos Aires, Argentina

English translation © 1987 by Orbis Books
Published by Orbis Books, Maryknoll, NY 10545
Manufactured in the United States of America
All rights reserved

Manuscript editor: William E. Jerman

Except for passages contained in quotations from another printed source, all Bible passages are from *The New American Bible*.

Library of Congress Cataloging in Publication Data

Lesbaupin, Ivo.
  Blessed are the persecuted.

  Translation of: A Bem-aventurançca da perseguição
  Bibliography: p.
  1. Persecution—History—Early church, ca. 30-600.
I. Title.
BR1604.2.L47   1987   272'.1   87-5746
ISBN 0-88344-562-X
ISBN 0-88344-561-1 (pbk.)

**To the memory of our brother,
Frei Tito de Alencar Lima, Martyr,
died, August 8, 1974**

These are the ones who have survived the great period of trial; they have washed their robes and made them white in the blood of the lamb.

It was this that brought them before God's throne:
    day and night they minister to him in his temple;
    he who sits on the throne will give them shelter.
Never again shall they know hunger or thirst,
    nor shall the sun or its heat beat down on them,
    for the Lamb on the throne will shepherd them.
He will lead them to springs of life-giving water,
    and God will wipe every tear from their eyes [Revelation
    7:14–17].

Tito had underlined this passage in his Bible.

76487

Contents

Introduction

This is an approach to the history of the primitive church through the prism of its persecution by the Roman empire. I shall examine the period extending from A.D. 64 to 313—that is, from the first persecution (under Nero) to the definitive cessation of persecution (with the Edict of Milan). I have made no attempt to take account of the innumerable theological quarrels, or the heresies, or even the councils of those times. My prime concern is with the reasons for the persecutions, their repercussions on the life of the church, the Christian resistance, and the theology developed by the victims of persecution in response to the concrete problems occasioned by what was going on.

From the first offensive of the empire, Christians confronted their oppressors courageously, testifying by their martyrdom to the primacy of their faith. The history of the first three centuries is watered by the blood of those who preferred freedom in death to an "accursed freedom" (p. 37).

With time and experience, the church gradually organized for the combat. The community took on a structure, distributed responsibilities, created means of communication—in a word, learned to live "underground." The witness of a faith, a hope, and a love that transcended the visible horizon of history, that despised death itself, had the effect that, despite all tribulations, the church continued to grow. In the second half of the third century, the church was a reality to be reckoned with in the empire, even quantitatively. And at the beginning of the fourth century, amid the most violent persecution of all, that empire had to make a public concession: "Nevertheless, because great numbers still persist in their opinions . . . we . . . have judged it fit to permit them again to be Christians" (p. 12.)

The purpose of this book is simply to seek to pierce the mystery of this tiny grain of wheat, of which Jesus had said that if it did not die, it would not fructify.

Chronology

Monarchy: to 509 B.C.
Republic: 509–30 B.C.
Empire: 30 B.C. to A.D. 476 (demise of the Roman empire of the West)

SUCCESSION OF ROMAN EMPERORS
TO CONSTANTINE

Emperors	Reign	Situation for Christians
Octavius Augustus	30–14 B.C.	[Birth of Christ: ca. 4 B.C.]
Tiberius Caesar	A.D. 14–37	[Life of Christ to ca. A.D. 30]
Caligula	37–41	
Claudius	41–54	
Nero	54–68	First Roman persecution: A.D. 64–68
Galba, Otho Vitellius	68–69	Tolerance
Flavius Vespasian	69–79	Tolerance
Titus	79–81	Tolerance

Domitian	81–96	Persecution: A.D. 95–96
Nerva	96–98	Tolerance
Trajan	98–117	Persecution
Hadrian	117–138	Persecution
Antoninus Pius	138–161	Persecution
Marcus Aurelius	161–180	Major Persecution
Commodus	180–193	Tolerance
Septimius Severus	193–211	First Imperial Edict against Christians: A.D. 202
Caracalla	211–217	Tolerance
Heliogabalus	218–222	Tolerance
Alexander Severus	222–235	Tolerance
Maximinus the Thracian	235–238	Persecution
Gordian	238–244	Tolerance
Philip the Arab	244–249	Tolerance
Decius	249–252	First general persecution: A.D. 250–251
Trebonius Gallus	251–253	General persecution
Valerian	253–260	General persecution: A.D. 257–260
Gallienus	260–268	Tolerance

Claudius II	268–270	Tolerance
Aurelian	270–275	Tolerance
Tacitus	275–276	Tolerance
Probus	276–282	Tolerance
Carus	283–284	Tolerance
Diocletian ⎫ Maximian ⎭	284–305	Persecution: A.D. 303–305
Galerius ⎫ Constantius Severus Maximinus Daia Maximian Maxentius Licinius Constantine ⎭	305–313	Persecution
Licinius ⎫ Constantine ⎭	313–324	Peace
Constantine	324–337	Peace

N.B.: Tolerance did not mean total peace: there were always local anti-Christian movements during these periods, of varying intensity, in which a certain number of martyrs were put to death.

CHAPTER 1

The Roman Empire and the Persecutions

CAUSE OF THE PERSECUTIONS: THE CHRISTIAN FAITH ROCKING THE FOUNDATIONS OF THE EMPIRE

The first three centuries of the Christian era were marked by persecutions of the infant church. From Christ to the Edict of Milan (A.D. 313), Christians were persecuted—first by the Jews, and then, beginning with Nero, by the Romans.

Until the burning of Rome in the year 64, the Roman empire peaceably accepted the presence of Christians. Indeed it did not easily distinguish Christians from Jews, and accorded both groups the same privilege: freedom to profess the religion of their native land, whatever it might be. The tribulations imposed by Jews on Christians were looked upon as dissension internal to Judaism (Acts 18:14-15; 25:19).

Paul's appeal to Caesar in the year 60, after two years of captivity in Caesarea, shows us that Christians did not yet see the empire as entertaining any hostility toward them. On the contrary, Paul hoped that the Roman authorities would deliver him from the machinations of the Jews (Acts 24:10-21; 25:10-11; 26:1-32). The emperor to whom he appealed was Nero, who shortly thereafter would turn against Christians. Paul was released in A.D. 63.

But the Book of Revelation, as early as around the year 95, when it was completed, gives another view of the empire. Christians could no longer legitimately submit to Roman authority, as Saint Paul had recommended (Rom. 13:1-7). The empire is described as

1

a wild beast coming from the sea. Rome was a great whore drunk with the blood of the martyrs. The situation had changed drastically.

The burning of Rome turned the people against Nero. All believed he had been responsible for the misfortune. Nero in turn blamed the Christians. He had precedent ready to hand: on the occasion of another fire, the magistrates, not finding the real culprits, had put the blame on a group of foreigners living in Rome. The fact that Christians were not Romans already cast suspicion on them: foreigners could wish for the downfall of Rome.

But why focus on Christians, instead of some other group? It may be that there was Jewish influence in singling out Christians as the ones to be harrassed. There were influential individuals of Judaizing tendencies in Nero's court. Jews did at times incite the Romans against Christians (see Acts 18:12–13).

At all events, there was already anti-Christian prejudice in the common mind. And there was need of a scapegoat to satisfy the discontent. What better one could be found than those to whom they were already hostile, albeit for other motives?

The Roman historian Tacitus (A.D. ca. 55–117) wrote:

> To suppress [the rumor that the fires that destroyed Rome had been deliberately set], Nero fabricated scapegoats—and punished with every refinement the notoriously depraved Christians (as they were popularly called). Their originator [one "Chrestos,"] had been executed in Tiberius' reign by the governor of Judaea, Pontius Pilatus. But in spite of this temporary setback the deadly *superstition* had broken out afresh, not only in Judaea (where the mischief had started) but even in Rome. All degraded and shameful practices collect and flourish in the capital.
>
> First, Nero had self-acknowledged Christians arrested. Then, on their information, large numbers of others were condemned—not so much for incendiarism as for their anti-social tendencies. Their deaths were made farcical. Dressed in wild animals' skins, they were torn to pieces by dogs, or crucified, or made into torches to be ignited after dark as substitutes for daylight [Tacitus, *Annals,* book 15, chap. 44, p. 354; emphasis added].

The victims of this persecution were many, and included Saint Peter and Saint Paul.

The passage from Tacitus reflects the allegations lodged against the Christians: abominations, superstition, and "hatred of the human race." The Jews had been accused of this last, originally due to the fact that the Jewish community had customs and practices that isolated it from the common life of the citizenry. Christians, on the other hand, did not hold themselves apart from the people—on the contrary, they eschewed any appearance of separatism. And yet, Christians had to abstain from observing idolatrous or pagan customs—certain public festivals (the theater, the circus), certain professions, and any profession of polytheism. After all, these involved violence done to one's neighbor (gladiatorial combat, or the pitting of human beings against wild beasts), disrespect for others (prostitution), or the worship of statues and human beings. Furthermore, Christians celebrated their worship in private and did not permit the participation of non-Christians, which created a certain air of mystery around their ceremonies.

The fact of *different* customs soon gave rise to the rumor of *inhumane* customs. Hence the accusations—incidentally, already lodged against the Jews—that Christians practiced *flagitia,* shameful abominations. The notion enjoyed common currency especially with the masses: Christians, in their secret meetings, were thought to adore an ass's head, practice infant sacrifice and cannibalism, and copulate incestuously in the course of their orgies.

It was their refusal to follow the masses in their pagan ritual practices that brought general hostility upon the heads of Christians. Faithful to the worship of the one true God, they refused to worship pagan gods, and especially the emperor, to whom they refused to ascribe divinity. For Christians, Christ was the only human being to be God. Accordingly, they were considered "atheists"—irreligious, sacrilegious. On numerous occasions the crowd, in a frenzy at seeing Christians enter the arena, would cry out, "Death to the atheists! Burn the godless ones!" It was precisely in its character as a different religion, and even more so as a new religion, that Christianity became the target of criticism, both on the part of the people and on that of the elite.

We shall be able to comprehend the anti-Christian attitude of the

Romans only in light of the nature of the religion of the age.

In classical antiquity, Greek as well as Roman, religion was the mainstay and basis of the polis, the city (understanding "city" as meaning the state, and politics). Religion was a function of the state, carried out by individuals specially designated for the purpose. "Interiority" played no role. Religion was a matter of formal ties and purely external cult. Politics was completely shot through with this "religion". It was impossible to separate one from the other. Worship formed the universal bond of union, held the whole of society together. As the home altar gathered together the members of a family, so the city was the confederacy of those who had the same gods as their protectors and performed the acts of religion at the same altar. To deny the gods was not only apostasy, but treason; worship was a civic function.

Still, Rome showed itself tolerant of the gods of its subject peoples. Each Roman conquest involved an addition to the pantheon. From its earliest beginnings, the empire had been invaded by numberless gods, ritual systems, and Eastern religions. Doubtless there were certain restrictions and prohibitive measures, but on the whole there was no hostility. At the basis of this tolerance was the principle that every people, every polis, had its own gods: the Roman conquest and annexation of that people entailed the appropriation of its territory and the political independence of its citizens, but not the supplanting of their religion. If the gods of Rome reached other lands it was in conjunction with other forms of Roman culture, and not by virtue of religious missions. At the same time, a minimal conformism with Roman religion was required of all.

So it went with the polytheistic systems of worship. But Judaism and Christianity, and they alone, were monotheistic. Still, Judaism was accorded the status of a lawful religion—a *religio licita*—in its quality of a national religion. Before as well as after the destruction of Jerusalem by Titus in the year 70, Yahweh was, for the Romans, a national god, the god of the Jewish people. The Jews scattered throughout the world were seen as resident aliens in the cities of the empire, and therefore had, in principle, the right to practice their particular cultus. Rome did not consider the Jews a danger to traditional religion. Indeed, they were granted certain privileges exempting them from civil obligations or duties incompatible with their religious faith. Judaism was the target of persecution only when it presented itself as a political threat to the empire (on the occasion of the messianic insurrections of the Zealots in A.D. 66 and 135, for example), or when it enjoyed religious expansion in the provinces (as with Septimius Severus and proselytism—see pages 8-9).

Christian theologian Tertullian observed that it was in the shadow of Judaism that Christianity was able to take its first steps without colliding with prevailing legislation. The situation changed when, in the eyes of Roman authority, a clear distinction appeared between Judaism and Christianity. Now it was a matter of a *new* religion (not an old one, like Judaism)—a "new and mischievous belief," as Suetonius called it (*Twelve Caesars,* p. 217). It was making its appearance in the empire with the *universal* mission of joining all human beings together in the same faith, and thus having a direct effect on paganism, the state religion and very foundation of the grandeur of the Roman empire. Its God was not a national god, and hence could be worshiped by everyone, Greek, Gaul, or African. Any citizen of the empire could become a Christian.

It was Octavius Augustus, founder of the empire, who introduced the divinization of the emperor. The emperor, now styled Supreme Pontiff—*Pontifex Maximus*—came to be called *Augustus, Divus, Divinus, Sol Invictus* ("Godly, Divine, Unconquered Sun") and *Dominus et Deus* ("Lord God"). The divinization of the emperor as an adjunct to religious life had the finality of developing the penetration, secure implantation, and cohesion of the empire everywhere. The worship of the emperor had unparalleled political effects, becoming the common denominator for all the inhabitants of the vast empire, so diversified in other respects.

Then too the Romans were convinced that they owed their prosperity and victory to fidelity to their gods. They regarded calamities as the doings of gods annoyed by some infidelity. And they considered that the gods were annoyed by the presence of persons who worshiped another God and denied them the worship that was their due. It was evident to all that the "atheism" of the Christians—their denial of the official gods, among which were now numbered Rome and Augustus (the emperor)—was more "mischievous" and threatening than other foreign religions. The discovery of a group of men and women who were the avowed enemies of the national gods aroused sentiments of hostility in the Roman soul. This was a threat to Roman tranquility. The Roman gods might be annoyed. It was a threat to Roman religion, as well, as Christianity expanded and gained new adherents. Accordingly, it was a political threat: the cohesion of the empire, based on religion and centering on the emperor, was in danger.

Christianity was held to be not only an illicit religion, but an illicit association as well—a *collegium illicitum*. But anyone entering into an outlawed association was guilty of a crime tantamount to lèse majesté, for which Roman law acknowledged no mitigating circumstance in the severity of its condemnation. This is the crime for which Cyprian, bishop of Carthage, was sentenced to be run through by the sword in the persecution carried on by Emperor Valerian:

> Galerius Maximus consulted with his advisory staff, and then with difficulty and reluctance spoke as follows: "You have long persisted in your sacrilegious views, and you have joined to yourself many other vicious men in a conspiracy. You have set yourself up as an enemy of the gods of Rome and of our religious practices; and the pious and venerable emperors Valerian and Gallienus Augusti and Valerian the most noble of Caesars have not been able to bring you back to the observance of their sacred rites.
>
> "Thus since you have been caught as the instigator and leader of a most atrocious crime, you will be an example for all those whom in your wickedness you have gathered to yourself. Discipline shall have its sanction in your blood."
>
> Then he read his decision from a tablet: "Thascius Cyprian is sentenced to die by the sword."
>
> The bishop Cyprian said: "Thanks be to God!" [*Acts of the Christian Martyrs,* "Acts of Cyprian," chap. 4, p. 173].

Another excellent example of the way in which Christians were regarded is to be found in Diocletian's amnesty of the year 303, which opened the prison gates to so many. The amnesty did not extend to Christians. These were held not as common criminals, but as *rebels.*

LEGISLATION ON CHRISTIANITY:
FROM ILLEGALITY TO PERSECUTION

Christianity was first juridically proscribed by Emperor Nero. From being a *superstitio illicita,* Christianity now became a *religio illicita.* We do not know with certainty how this proscription was juridically established. Tertullian states that Nero issued a legal decree, the *institutum neronianum,* to the following effect: *ut Christiani non sint*—"Let there not be Christians" (Tertullian, *Apologeticum,* 5). In any case, the fact is that Christianity came to be considered juridically criminal.

The emperors of the first two centuries did not initiate general persecutions. The earliest persecutions were the outcome of local movements and limited popular initiatives, with the approval, merely, of the magistracy. It was the people who called for persecution, frequently engaging in it themselves and rendering it more cruel, and incessantly provoking the hostility of emperors and magistrates against Christians. Of course, it was precisely among the popular classes that Christianity enjoyed its greatest expansion. The members of those classes, however, who had not been converted, usually the majority, were vexed by the Christians' aversion to traditional opinions and ancient beliefs. Furthermore, the popular ranks included both fallen disciples and fanatical adversaries. The latter found it altogether legitimate to punish anyone who refused to follow the traditional norms of society. They judged it their obligation, in loyalty to the gods, to eliminate Christians. The magistrates, in turn, were nearly always extremely solicitous when it came to respecting the demands of the multitudes, especially when these multitudes were gathered in the stadium. Imperial rescripts of the second century sought chiefly to bridle the popular frenzy, and relied on the magistrates to keep the opportunity for these tumults to a minimum.

Meanwhile, Christianity continued to be illegal. Around A.D. 112, Pliny the Younger, governor of Bithynia, consulted the Emperor Trajan as to what attitude he ought to take with regard to Christians. Trajan responded with a rescript that became the jurisprudential norm in the matter for the whole second century. The rescript determined substantially the following:

1. Governmental authority ought not to initiate persecutions. It need not go looking for Christians.

2. Persons denounced as Christians and declaring themselves not to be such, or henceforward not to be such, and giving evidence of their sincerity through an act of worship of the gods, are to be exonerated.

3. Persons professing Christianity are to be sentenced.

4. Anonymous denunciations are not to be admitted (see Daniélou and Marrou, *First Six Hundred Years,* p. 85).

The Emperor Hadrian, in the year 124, supplied some further prescriptions. Denunciations were to be accompanied by legal evidence. Acclamation—the simple cries of the multitudes—had no legal force. And false informers were to be punished (see ibid., p. 87).

The legal discipline regarding Christians in the first two centuries, then, was: a legal procedure could always be undertaken against publicly professed Christians or Christians denounced as such in juridical form. The latter was a common occurrence indeed, in view of the prevailing hostility. In this period, then, the situation for Christians was one of considerable insecurity.

We might call this discipline one of "diffuse persecution." Now it would break out here, now there—persecution today, toleration tomorrow. Indeed, under various emperors, there were relatively prolonged periods of toleration. Persecution on the local level, however, occasionally reached levels of great intensity.

For, when all was said and done, it was a crime to be a Christian. But it was a crime sui generis. Those who committed it were not to be ferreted out. And yet, simply the fact of being a Christian was an infringement of the law. Those who were accused of this crime and confessed to it would have to be punished. If they denied the charge, exoneration was automatic, and a word or gesture would suffice.

With Septimius Severus, in the year 202, a new discipline was initiated, to be maintained by a number of his successors: public authority, in circumstances that will vary, now assumed the *initiative* for persecutions. Trajan's rule—not to "go looking for Christians"—has been abandoned. The era of persecution by edict has begun. Correlatively, persecution based on the denunciation of individuals will become more rare, to the point where it will eventually cease altogether.

From the beginning of the third century to the beginning of the fourth, the church suffered the shock of sudden and violent explosions. A persecution would flare up and then die down. Each new collapse was a milestone in the waning of a pagan empire vis-à-vis a waxing Christianity. In between were periods, sometimes long ones, of peace, which, although shaken from time to time by the application of the old discipline, tended to become more and more firm and lasting.

In the year 202 Severus issued an edict prohibiting Christians and Jews from proselytizing—from seeking to propagate their respective religions. This was the first imperial edict directed against the church. The measure was motivated by concern for the empire: the advance of Christian (and Jewish) propaganda alarmed the Roman authority, which saw in it a threat to the imperial order through the undermining of traditional religion. But, let it be observed, the decree was not directed against those who were already Christians. It sought to stem the tide of Christianity. And hence, generally speaking, bishops were not especially uneasy during this period. Only those persons were affected by this persecution who were preparing for baptism ("catechumens"), those who had recently received baptism ("neophytes"), and those charged with their preparation ("catechists"). The crime with which this new edict was concerned, then, was that of seeking to *become* a Christian. However, previous legislation was not abrogated. Being a Christian continued to be a punishable crime in instances of a denunciation.

Only from about the middle of the third century do we find a full-blown discipline of persecution, complete with carefully constructed edicts, for the purpose of the *systematic extermination of Christianity*. The first emperor to decree a general persecution of Christians was Decius. Despite its brief duration (A.D. 250–251), Decius's persecution was unparalleled, both in its intensity and in its extent. The emperor's objective, like that of Severus before him, was to strengthen Roman unity by reinforcing its religious focus. Hence his preoccupation with making apostates rather than martyrs. The edict of Decius provided that every citizen of the empire must offer sacrifice to the gods of Rome. After having performed the sacrificial rite, the citizen in question was to receive a certificate, a *libellus,* attesting to compliance with the law and the discharge of the obligation therein provided, with the person's name and date and the words: "Sacrifice Duly Offered: . . . I have always sacrificed to the gods, and now in Your Presence, in compliance with what is ordered in the edict, I have sacrificed, have offered libations, and have participated in the sacred banquet; wherefore I beg Your certification to this effect."

The persecution was meticulously organized. The prisons filled with Christians. The chief victim was Pope Fabian, who died a martyr on January 20, A.D. 250. Bishops, in their capacity as heads of churches, were the special victims of the edict.

Valerian (A.D. 253–260), after a period of peace, unleashed a new persecution, in the year 257, at the instigation of his finance minister Macrianus.

A special characteristic of Valerian's persecution was the part played in it by a certain pagan mystique that was animated by a passionate hatred of Christianity. Macrianus was an important and influential member of certain pagan confraternities originating in Egypt. He also realized that, in view of the worsening financial situation of the empire, the undertaking would provide a source of income. Macrianus was the first statesman to advocate an anti-Christian project for the purpose of revenue. Ecclesiastical property at the time had assumed considerable proportions, and part of the Roman aristocracy had now come into the church.

Valerian's first edict, in August 257, was aimed especially at the clergy—the bishops, presbyters or priests, and deacons—of whom recognition of the gods of the empire was stipulated, through an act of ritual sacrifice. Simultaneously, however, its dispositions affected all the faithful as well, in that it forbade them, under threat of capital punishment, to celebrate their own worship or meet in their cemeteries. Valerian's second edict provided for the immediate execution of such members of the clergy who had not offered sacrifice, and the confiscation of the goods of Christians of the upper classes. The persecutions of Valerian and Decius were the most violent of the third century.

Gallienus, Valerian's successor, reestablished the discipline of toleration, a period of peace that would end only forty years later, under Diocletian. Gallienus's provisions authorized Christian worship, ordered the restoration of churches, and permitted Christians to repossess their cemeteries. These provisions were not yet the transformation of Christianity into a *religio licita,* but they did constitute the recognition of a fact: the development of the church, its penetration of the elite, and its quantitative growth was something that the state could no longer ignore.

Diocletian initiated his persecution only after some twenty years of his reign, at the instigation of his colleague, Caesar Galerius. Here was the last, longest, and most violent of the persecutions, lasting from A.D. 303 to 313. Some years before, A.D. 297, expurgation of Christians from the Roman army had begun.

The empire had known a terrible crisis in the third century, in which it had threatened to founder. From 235 to 285, extraterritorial enemies threatened its frontiers; within, instability, civil war, economic difficulties, and anarchy threatened as well. Diocletian undertook the task of rescuing the empire, and to this end he made use of coercion and violence.

The new empire was a genuine totalitarian state, in the modern sense of the word—a state that seeks to subject to its authority all the energies of all its subjects, unifying them by absorbing them (Daniélou and Marrou, *First Six Hundred Years,* pp. 227–30). The authority of the head of state was characterized in absolutist terms. Ever since the time of Augustus, there had been a religious element in the structure of imperial authority. With the new regime this characteristic became still more salient. Diocletian's reliance on the religious traditions of ancient Rome, together with his ideal, so passionately maintained, of a unity and cohesiveness, which he expressed in all his policies, necessarily led to a collision of the pagan empire and the Christian religion.

Four edicts appeared in quick succession—in less than a year, from February 24, 303, to January or February of the year 304. The first edict bore chiefly upon public worship. It provided for the destruction of churches, the burning of sacred scriptures and liturgical books, and the confiscation of sacred vessels. Christians came to be excluded from public functions and deprived of certain civil rights. The second edict ordered the imprisonment of the heads of all of the churches. The third prescribed the release of those who should offer sacrifice, and the torture of those who would not. The fourth, as in the time of Decius, obliged all the inhabitants of the empire, under pain of torture, prison, and death, to offer sacrifice to the imperial gods. Again the prisons filled with Christians, and again, especially in the first year of the persecution, it was the members of the clergy who were its principal victims. Rome was without a pope for four consecutive years.

During the ten years of its duration, however, the persecution was repeatedly interrupted, and its intensity varied from place to place. In the regions of the empire under Constantius (and later under Constantine)—Gaul, Britain, and Spain—only the first edict was applied, and without great enthusiasm. In the rest of the West the persecution was of brief duration, by and large no longer than two years. In the East, however—Libya, Egypt, Palestine, Syria, even Illyricum—it was a great deal more severe, lasting, with certain respites, until spring of the year 313. It was remarkable for the violence of its tortures, the number of its martyrs, and the cruel deaths to which they were subjected.

Beginning its eighth year, the persecution began to subside (A.D. 310–311). In 311, Galerius issued an edict recognizing the uselessness of the persecution in view of the unflagging resistance of the Christians:

> After the publication of our edict, ordaining the Christians to betake themselves to the observance of the ancient institutions, many of them were subdued through the fear of danger, and moreover many of them were exposed to jeopardy; nevertheless, because *great numbers* still persist in their opinions . . . we . . . have judged it fit to permit them again to be Christians, and to establish the places of their religious assemblies [Lactantius, *Of the Manner in Which the Persecutors Died,* p. 315].

Maximinus Daia refused to accept this resolution, and soon pursued the persecution of Christians implacably. Only after his defeat by Licinius, April 30, 313, did he grant the Christians complete freedom. It was the so-called Edict of Milan, of June 13, 313, that put a definitive end to the Roman persecution of Christians. It was promulgated by Licinius in Nicomedia. Constantine and Licinius had met earlier in Milan and come to an agreement. The edict granted religious liberty to all (including those of other religions), and decreed the restitution of churches and other confiscated properties.

SUMMARY: TWO HUNDRED FIFTY YEARS OF PERSECUTION

Until the reign of Septimius Severus, Roman legal discipline regarding Christians was based on the jurisprudence of Trajan. With Severus began the imperial edicts against Christianity. Decius decreed the first general persecution. The discipline inaugurated by Decius was carried to its ultimate consequences by Diocletian.

The persecution extended, then, in greater and lesser degrees of intensity, for two and one-half centuries, and reached throughout the length and breadth of the empire. It was not constant, but intermittent. Under various emperors it was limited to particular times and particular places. The emperors most remarkable for their hostility to Christianity generally only launched their persecutions at the end of their respective reigns, and even then these did not rage with the same savagery in all places at the same time, but might be particularly intense in one locale and nonexistent in another. Even in the general persecutions, the sheer geographical extent of the empire prevented the law from being applied with equal severity everywhere.

During the whole age of the persecutions, however, Christians lived in permanent insecurity, and suffered the hostility of the people. Christians were technically outlaws, always and everywhere, until the Edict of Milan. Even in times of truce and calm, when the Christian community could breathe a bit easier, no judge could ever refuse to punish them if they were denounced.

Broadly speaking, we may say, then, that Christians from A.D. 64 to 313 fared as follows.

first century: 6 years of persecution, 30 of toleration
second century: 86 years of persecution, 14 of toleration
third century: 24 years of persecution, 76 of toleration
fourth century: 13 years of persecution

The church knew 129 years of persecution and 120 of tranquility. The distribution of the years of persecution shows that all generations experienced the drama of martyrdom, and had to be prepared for it. All writers of the age, pagan and Christian alike, are unanimous in their recognition of the great number of martyrs. According to the data we have, and despite their incompleteness, the total number of martyrs may be calculated to have been at least one hundred thousand, and probably less than two hundred thousand.

But the number of the martyrs fails to provide a realistic image of the persecutions, because for each martyr there were perhaps a hundred other Christians who suffered the confiscation of their goods and property, imprisonment, torture, banishment, or condemnation to slave labor in the mines.

CHAPTER 2

Life of the Church: Faith and Witness

GENERAL VIEW: THE CHURCH ORGANIZED FOR RESISTANCE

The Roman empire persecuted Christianity because it saw in it a religion that, owing to its political consequences, must be considered an enemy religion. And so it burned the sacred books, destroyed the churches, obstructed proselytism, and forbade assemblies and even the visiting of cemeteries (which were places of assembly). The principal aim was to force Christians to return to paganism. Apostasy (or "recovery," depending on the viewpoint) was the prime objective.

The first victims of nearly every persecution were the leaders, the heads of the communities: popes and bishops above all, then priests and deacons. It was hoped that the apostasy of leaders would occasion a fall into discouragement and apostasy on the part of followers. However, the leaders were the most firm and constant in the profession of their faith, and bishops who yielded were promptly rejected by their communities (Lebreton and Zeiller, *De la fin du IIe. siècle,* p. 439). But of course not only the bishops were ready for martyrdom. The whole community had to face this possibility.

Beginning with Trajan, the persecutions included a test of whether citizens were Christian: they were required to offer sacrifice to the Roman gods or the emperor. In some of the persecutions, all citizens were required to take this test. And Christians, from the catechumens to the elderly, children, women, and young persons, bore witness to their faith, in court and by martyrdom. In other words, the laity had to have the same attitudes of Christian life as the clergy. And it was largely so. True, there were many apostasies, especially in the third century, when Christians had become fairly numerous, and in persecutions following upon a long period of tranquility (Decius's persecution, twelve years after that of Maximinus the Thracian; Diocletian's, forty-three years after Valerian's). But there were also a large number of confessors and martyrs.

Confessors were those who had "confessed" or professed their faith in Christ in prison, even under torture, but without dying for the faith, and therefore without martyrdom in the strict sense of the word. Their courage often rivaled that of the martyrs themselves.

In some communities almost all the accused held firm. There were even cases in which, following the imprisonment of their bishop, Christians presented themselves to the governor as a group and declared that they were indeed Christians, and ready to suffer the same consequences as their shepherd (Lebreton and Zeiller, ibid., p. 151).

The persecutions moved the church to organize. Christians were being interrogated, tortured, sentenced to prison or forced labor in the mines, exiled, and martyred. Those who exercised some function of leaderhsip in the community—bishops, presbyters, deacons, subdeacons, lectors, exorcists—assumed the responsibility of coordinating this organization. If the bishop was imprisoned, the college of presbyters assumed the direction of the community. It was the duty of the priests, even at the risk of prison or death, to come to the assistance of brothers and sisters who were in danger and stood in need of some material, moral, or spiritual support. Certain deacons were specially designated to visit imprisoned Christians, as well as to gather up and bury the bodies of the martyrs. These were dangerous duties. The magistrate would frequently forbid anyone to approach the imprisoned, as well as the corpses of the martyrs. There is a reference to this practice in the Book of Revelation (11:9). There was a mutual assistance fund, to provide for the needs of Christians in prison, exile, hiding, or flight.

In his anti-Christian work, *De Morte Peregrini,* Lucian of Samosata has left us a testimonial of the fellowship that characterized at least one local church:

> Well, when he [Peregrinus] had been imprisoned, the Christians, regarding the incident as a calamity, left nothing undone in the effort to rescue him. Then, as this was impossible, every other form of attention was shown him, not in any casual way but with assiduity; and from the very break of day aged widows and orphaned children could be seen waiting near the prison, while their officials even slept inside with him after bribing the guards. Then elaborate meals were brought in, and sacred books of theirs were read aloud [Lucian, *The Passing of Peregrinus,* no. 12, p. 13].

Certain members of the community were designated to serve those working in the mines, or in exile, and to provide for the maintenance of their contact with the community. The persons so designated ran the risk of condemnation to the same penalties or worse. The bishops, shepherds of an afflicted flock, sought to maintain the resolution and cohesion of the community, inspired the confessors, encouraged the faith, hope, and love of the faithful, saw to the continuation of the various services, and took care that no one was abandoned. "Whether widows or the confined who cannot support themselves or those who are in prison or excluded from their own dwellings, they ought, indeed, to have some to minister to them" (Letter from the Presbyters of Rome to the church of Carthage, in Cyprian, *Letters,* 8, no. 3, p. 22).

The community accorded martyrs and confessors a special status. The confessors' task was to intercede, along with the community, for those who had apostatized, so that they might be received back into the community. Once the persecution was over, the choice of a leader in the community tended to fall on confessors, in their quality as persons who had demonstrated the firmness of their faith in time of trial.

Even in periods when pagan hostility burst forth in all its savagery, conversions continued. The vitality of the church and of the Christian witness must have been considerable. Pagans who would apply for baptism were prepared in the "catechumenate," which was quite demanding, especially from about the middle of the second century. Candidates were admitted to baptism only after three years of preparation, at the end of which time they had to demonstrate not only a solid foundation in Christian doctrine, but, by their manner of life, the Christian dispositions they now professed to assume. The testimony of the community concerning their behavior was a factor in the decision to accept them or not. Catechesis took account of the difficult times: "At the same time as being instructed for baptisms, catechumens were instructed for martyrdom, feeling not the slightest temptation or disturbance in their profession of the living God in the face of the various manners of death they were to suffer" (Homily on Jer. 4:3, cited in *Actas de los Mártires,* p. 39). So wrote Origen, a catechist at the age of eighteen during the persecution of Septimius Severus. Christian formation must have been adequate: often enough, adolescents of both sexes conducted themselves impeccably in the face of interrogation, torture, and martyrdom.

During periods of persecution, it became difficult to assemble the community for worship. Christians continued to use their cemeteries for their liturgical meetings, both in the open air and in the catacombs. These served for their celebration of the eucharistic sacrifice, the veneration of the martyrs, and common prayer. The witness of sisters and brothers in captivity for the faith, or martyred, was always recalled and celebrated as fidelity to the example of Christ. The martyrs were honored not as dead, but as living, united with the celebrants as permanent intercessors before the throne of God.

Christians constituted the minority in communities of the empire during the first two centuries, with the possible exception of Asia Minor, where the church had enjoyed the most expansion. Toward the end of the second century its growth elsewhere as well was remarkable enough to attract the notice of the imperial authority. Until then, Christianity had been basically a religion of the poor and lowly, the enslaved—"workers in wool and leather, and fullers," as Celsus would sneer, ca. 177–180 (Origen, *Against Celsus,* book 3, chap. 55, p. 486). The conversion of members of the elite had always been difficult. The aristocracy and the intelligentsia looked on Christianity with contempt, and few were the conversions to Christianity from those circles.

But from about the middle of the third century Christianity

began to infiltrate new social strata. Now Christianity began to appear as the religion of certain members of the ruling class. It was likewise about this time that Christianity enjoyed its greatest quantitative expansion. All this influenced the behavior of the church during periods of persecution.

THE CATACOMBS: CREATIVE RESISTANCE

There were no Christian cemeteries until the end of the first century. When they finally appeared, they were at first established on the private property of wealthy families who had been converted and placed their own funerary domains at the disposition of their brothers and sisters in Christ. Christians had two types of cemeteries—above ground and underground. The latter were called crypts, hypogees, or "catacombs"—a word that originally denoted only one of these underground galleries, located near a depression in the overhead terrain and therefore said to be *ad catacumbas,* "at the hollow," but which later came to be used for them all.

The use of underground cemeteries was not peculiar to Christians. It had been the practice of the Egyptians and Phoenicians, and was later imitated by the Jews. Some Roman family cemeteries were in the nature of miniature catacombs.

What was remarkable about the Christian catacombs was their extent. Some had all the features of subterranean cities. They were to be found in Rome, Naples, Sicily, Tuscany, northern Africa, and Asia Minor (Turkey). The most extensive remains are in Rome. Some of the tunnels there are three stories high and 25 meters deep. Their total length is many hundreds of kilometers. The catacomb of Saint Sabina alone is 1,600 meters in length, with a total area of 16,475 square meters.

Pagans customarily celebrated a ritual funeral banquet. Christians used to gather in prayer, in the company of the dead, to pray and perform their liturgical ceremonies in their cemeteries. The cult of the martyrs developed early. Then the insecurity in which Christians had to live, always present and sometimes drastic, led them to transform the catacombs into places of worship. Roman legislation accorded special protection to funerary properties. It was always safer to meet in a cemetery. As the persecutions continued, and grew in extent and intensity, Christians were motivated to extend the catacombs, chiefly from about the middle of the second century to the end of the third.

In normal times worship was held in private homes, or, beginning in the third century, in buildings specially dedicated to worship. Churches, as such, appeared only in the latter half of the third century. In critical times, however, liturgical life became centered in the catacombs. On the occasion of the systematic violence of the third century, the catacombs were furnished as places of refuge, with networks of tunnels, false doors, and secret exits to neighboring quarries. These "cities of the dead" reflect the lifestyle of the early Christians, their sense of community, their patient resistance, their creativity.

LEGISLATION OF OPPRESSION: DETENTION, TRIAL, AND PUNISHMENT

The initiation of criminal legal proceedings was not a matter of public responsibility in ancient Roman law. Today when a crime is committed, a public prosecutor has the obligation to initiate judicial procedures. In Roman antiquity the accusation was normally lodged by a private citizen, who had also to present evidence of the crime. In the absence of a private denunciation, a judge magistrate had discretionary power to initiate proceedings, but was under no obligation to do so, not even in the case of notorious criminality. Trajan had expressly forbidden magistrates to do so in the case of Christians. A typical example was that of Justin, a convert to Christianity about the year 130, who became the great apologist for Christianity. He was known in Rome as a Christian; indeed, he conducted a school, at a time when Christians were being executed for their faith. Still, for years he was left in peace. Only when a private denunciation was lodged against him was he arrested and martyred (A.D. 165).

In fact, Christians were visited in prison not only by the members of their families, but also by deacons and priests, who even celebrated the eucharistic sacrifice with them, thereby proclaiming themselves guilty of the same crime—that of being a Christian. Prison officials and magistrates must have known that such visitors were Christians, indeed that they performed certain official church functions. Or again, prisoners would dictate letters to bishops and other Christians, which of course was evidence that there still were Christians at large. But until they were formally denounced, they remained at liberty.

Their crime was simply that of being a Christian. Once anyone had professed the Christian faith, therefore, he or she could be judged and sentenced without further ado. There was no need of directives to this effect, testimony, or oaths. Being a Christian was a crime for which there was no legitimate defense. Frequently, in order to force an apostasy—either an explicit denial of the Christian faith or sacrifice to the gods—magistrates might direct that the accused be subjected to torture. Only after they were convicted— and the trial might go on for years—was a sentence drawn up and pronounced.

There was a variety of punishments to which a convicted Christian might be sentenced:

A. Capital Punishment
   1. Crucifixion
   2. Burning
   3. Decapitation
   4. Torture—extremely varied in kind, culminating in death
   5. Being thrown to the beasts in the arena. It was the custom, on certain days and on certain civic occasions, to provide the people with spectacles in the "circus," a circular stadium encompassing an *arena,* "the sand." The main attraction of these spectacles was the combat between gladiators ("swordsmen") or between gladiators and wild beasts. Criminals under capital sentence were thrown to the beasts, with or without some paltry means of defense, such as a sword, and, on the occasion of the persecutions, these criminals included Christians. The beasts unleashed upon the victims included every kind of ferocious animal—from bulls and wild boars to bears, leopards, and lions. Victims did not always die in the encounter, in which case they were decapitated.
B. Exile (*Relegatio)*
C. Forced labor in the mines

Torture

> The [one] who holds out till the end is the one who will come through safe [Mark 13:13].

The purpose of torture was to force Christians to deny their faith. Another purpose was to move them to denounce other Christians, giving their names and telling where they might be found.

The accused would be stripped, bound to a column, and scourged with rods, or with whips of rope tipped with lead. In frequent use was the rack, consisting of a wooden frame, supported on four legs and long enough to hold a person placed up on it spread-eagle. At its corners were chains or ropes attached to wheels. The victim was extended on the rack face upward, with hands and feet attached to the wheels by means of the ropes. The wheels were turned so as to tighten the ropes and stretch the whole body. Joints might be dislocated in this way. This was one of the more severe tortures.

Also used were iron combs, forks, and claws, for tearing all parts of the body, red-hot irons and gridirons for burning the flesh, as well as melted lead or boiling oil, which was slowly poured over the most delicate areas of the body.

Phileas, bishop of Tmuis, wrote a letter from prison. He describes for his flock the tortures to which his companions in prison were subjected:

> When all who wished to insult them had complete freedom to do so, some struck them with clubs, others with rods, others with scourges, others, again, with straps, and others with ropes. And the sight of their tortures was varied and possessed of much malice within it. . . . Others were raised on high and hung from the porch by one hand, suffering the most terrible of all pain through the stretching of their joints and limbs. . . . And this they endured, not as long as the governor talked or was at leisure with them, but almost throughout the entire day. For . . . if perchance anyone being overcome by the tortures seemed to be giving in . . . he commanded them to approach also with bonds mercilessly,

and when after this they were at the last gasp, to arrange them upon the ground and drag them off [Eusebius, *Ecclesiastical History,* book 8, chap. 10, pp. 181–82].

No consideration whatever was shown age, sex, or social status. The elderly, women, adolescents, and even children suffered the same torments. Women, in addition to the tortures just listed, might be raped. . . . "The judge (his name was Aquila) imposed severe punishments on her entire body and finally threatened to hand her over to the gladiators for bodily abuse" (ibid., book 6, chap. 5, p. 13).

Eusebius, bishop of Caesarea in Palestine, was a Christian historian, and testifies to the events of the persecution of Diocletian. He is the principal source for the history of the primitive church, especially in the ten books of his *Ecclesiastical History.* Eusebius gives the following description of torture during Diocletian's persecution:

> Why should I now make mention by name of the rest or number the multitude of the men or picture the various sufferings of the wonderful martyrs, sometimes slaughtered with the axe, as happened to those in Arabia, sometimes having their legs broken, as fell to the lot of those in Cappadocia, and on some occasions being raised on high by the feet with heads down and, when a slow fire was lit underneath them, choking to death by the smoke sent out from the burning wood, as was visited upon them in Mesopotamia, sometimes having their noses and ears and hands mutilated, and the other limbs and parts of the body cut to pieces, as took place in Alexandria?
>
> Why should we rekindle the memory of those in Antioch who were roasted on hot grates, not unto death but with a view to a lingering punishment, and of others who let their right hand down into the very fire sooner than touch the abominable sacrifice? . . .
>
> And in Pontus [Turkey] others suffered in a manner frightful to hear: the fingers of both hands were pierced through by sharp reeds under the tips of the nails [ibid., book 8, chap. 12, pp. 184–86].

Magistrates would even have wedges or chains put into the mouth of a Christian to keep it open long enough to force the victim to drink the wine of Roman sacrificial libations.

Among various mutilations practiced, there was castration.

The main purpose of torture was to "break down" the accused, to make them "give in" or yield. A duel would often take place between the accused and the magistrate. The judge would look on the "examination" as a challenge of his skill. Lactantius recounts that a governor of Bithynia boasted that he had succeeded in breaking down a Christian who had resisted for two years—as if the governor had finally triumphed over a barbarian nation. When the victim remained steadfast, the judge would become enraged and desperate: he could look upon his failure only as a defeat in a very important contest. In order to defeat the accused, it was important to prolong their life as long as possible, alternating torture sessions and respite—physical and psychological torture, respectively—in a process in which imprisonment itself played a role.

And so a true *ars dolorum* developed—an art of torture, or what today is called "scientific torture." Instruments and techniques for provoking intense, constant pain without causing the victim's death were perfected. Next the importance of an interval between torture sessions was discovered, to afford victims time to reflect on the tortures just past and to anticipate those to come, in the hope that they would fail to continue to bear up under them. A respite was psychologically important, then. It was discovered to be important to keep the victim alive and yet to close off all hope of diminution or interruption of the torment through release or death. This had to be made clear. "If you yield, the torture will be over and you shall be released. If you do not yield, the torture will be continued, and become ever more severe." The calculation was that as victims came to grasp the situation, they would be led to despair, then panic, and would finally be willing to yield. And indeed this rigorously methodical procedure sometimes obtained the desired results—exhaustion, despair, and the collapse of the victims' resistance (especially their psychic resistance, physical resistance having been broken in a brief time, as the victim's whole body was completely torn and lacerated). Some, then, lost the duel. But countless others prevailed and, each time the tortures would recommence, gave evidence of redoubled fortitude.

It should be observed here that two auxiliary methods were made use of. The first consisted in announcing that someone had offered Roman sacrifice—when in fact it was not true. There were even occasions when Christians were simply taken to a non-Christian altar and the public was led to believe that they offered sacrifice there. The objective was to have the person in question rejected by the Christian community, to wound the morale of that community, and to sow confusion. The second method consisted in the public defamation of Christians. Persons would be bribed or tortured to obtain their testimony to alleged heinous practices of Christians. A spurious *Acts of Pilate* appeared, maligning and defiling the historical personage of Christ, with the order that it be published and taught in the schools.

Prison: School of Confessors and Martyrs

Theoretically the empire did not sentence culprits to imprisonment. The purpose of prison was preventive detention, which could be of long duration, while the accused were awaiting trial. In practice, there were illegal sentences of imprisonment. At all events, alleged criminals often spent months and even years in prison, awaiting sentencing.

Especially during the persectuion of Decius, imprisonment was relied on as a means of breaking an individual's resistance. Life in the dungeons, with their darkness, stench, promiscuity, and crowds of persons of the worst ilk, was terrible. Many died there, be it for lack of medical assistance, or even by suffocation. There were no hygienic facilities whatever, and rations were unspeakably inadequate.

But worse still were the jails, tombs of eternal night, where prisoners were encased in wooden boxes. "The days we passed there and the nights we endured cannot be expressed in human words. The torments we suffered in prison go beyond anything we could describe." And yet, in the horrors of the night, the light of faith seemed bright as day ("Acts of Montanus and Lucius," in *Acts of the Christian Martyrs,* pp. 217–19).

As if the place itself were not torment enough, prison had its special tortures. Convicts were chained, with special weight on foot chains, or, worse, were placed in stocks (the *lignum,* or *nervus*), a wooden pedestal having holes at regular intervals in which a prisoner's feet could be locked. The agony suffered was in proportion to the distance the feet were spread: maximum distance appears to have been that of the "fifth hole," which caused death by rupture of the trunk under its own weight. The instrument is frequently cited in the *Acts of the Martyrs.* (See also Acts 16:24–*tous podas esphalisato auton eis to xulon.*)

In addition, executioners might have recourse to affliction by hunger and thirst. "We were ordered, according to the command of the emperor, to be killed by hunger and thirst; and we were shut up in two cells. . . . The fire from the effect of our affliction was so intolerable that no one could bear it" (Letter of Lucian, a confessor in prison in Carthage, in Cyprian, *Letters,* 22, no. 2, p. 60).

Forced labor in the mines was an unremitting horror, even apart from the fact that it was always a life sentence. The condemned were sentenced to labor in quarries, gold mines, silver mines, lead mines, and copper mines. Often this punishment included mutilation in the form of the severing of the tendons of the left knee and the putting out of the right eye. Eusebius wrote that Christians "were condemned to the copper mines in the province, not so much for service as for mistreatment and hardship" (*Ecclesiastical History,* book 8, chap. 12, p. 187).

. The authorities were occasionally found to credit allegations of infanticide, incest, and magic lodged against Christians by the masses. In these instances even those who had denied the faith remained in prison, accused of these common-law delicts. But there was a striking difference in comportment between those who had remained firm in the confession of the faith and those who had yielded:

> The joy of martyrdom and the hope of what was promised and the love toward Christ and the Spirit of the Father lightened the burden of [those who had confessed Christ], but conscience greatly punished [those who had denied him], so that their faces were conspicuous among all the rest when

they were led out. The former came forth gladly, with glory and much grace mingled on their faces, so that even their fetters rested about them as a becoming ornament . . . but the others were downcast and depressed and ugly and filled with every unseemliness; moreover, they were insulted by the heathen as ignoble and unmanly. . . . Now, when the others beheld this [those who had not been arrested], they were made firm, and those who were [thereupon] arrested confessed without hesitation, giving no thought to the arguments of the Devil [Letter of the community of Lyons to the churches of Asia Minor and Phrygia, in Eusebius, *Ecclesiastical History,* book 5, chap. 1, pp. 280–81].

But the Christians in the cells did not abandon those who had yielded. They took into consideration that their betrayal had been out of fear, and so they undertook to encourage them again, to awaken in them a deeper faith, a greater hope, a more radical love, capable of giving them the mettle to withstand the trial, to pass the test. And so, with time, and the patience of the confessors, who, physically weakened and wounded themselves, exhorted them to gain control over themselves and stand tall again, many returned to Christianity more firmly and courageously than ever. Interrogated anew, they withstood the barbarities. "And Christ was greatly glorified in those who, though they had formerly denied, now, contrary to the expectation of the heathen, confessed. For they were examined privately as if, indeed, they were to be set free, but on confessing they were added to the list of the martyrs" (ibid., p. 284).

Indeed the community had a principle: never to give up on anyone who had fallen. There was always the possibility of recovery:

> You see, therefore, Brethren, that you also ought to do this, so that even those who have fallen, correcting their minds by your exhortation, may confess, if they should be taken again, in order that they may be able to correct their former error [Letter of the presbyters of Rome to the church of Carthage, in Cyprian, *Letters,* 8, no. 3, p. 22].

In fact there was a pragmatic reason: "lest, if they should be abandoned by us, they should become worse" (ibid.).

Indeed, those who had fallen would sink into feelings of guilt and disorientation such that would lead them to fall all the more seriously. To give up on them now meant, literally, to allow them to "become worse"—to allow them to sink to such a point of degradation as themselves to become enemies of the Christians, and collaborators with the persecutors, which actually occurred in a number of cases. Support and assistance, on the contrary, afforded them an opportunity to recover their balance, to recover an awareness of their former option, of their responsibility, and thus enabled them—if they were disposed to this renewal—to comport themselves with steadfastness. Of course, they were not always so disposed. They might already have gone over to the other side.

Captive Christians were a most remarkable source of inspiration and oneness for their communities. Everywhere the sisters and brothers at liberty made it a point to visit those in prison, to raise their spirits, to renew and deepen the wellspring of their joy, their peace, their courage. The confessors, for their part, were tireless in writing their communities letters of encouragement, depositions concerning what had happened with themselves in prison, how the power of the Spirit had been made manifest in them, inspiring them to martyrdom. The correspondence between the captives and the free was plenteous. It was the great communications medium. Bishop Cyprian, for example, during the persecution of Decius, actually managed to direct the church of Carthage from his hiding-place beyond the confines of the city. There he sent and received messages, wrote letters of support to confessors, gave orders to priests, deacons, and laity. Simultaneously the confessors encouraged him, making suggestions, and exchanging ideas with him about attitudes to be assumed toward certain questions.

Some prisoners even managed to keep a journal, in order to preserve every last detail, discovery, or testimonial of those days that they considered to be days of an intense experience of communion with Christ. The *Acts of Perpetua and Felicity* is in part the work of these two holy women martyrs themselves.

The confessors formed a community. They often gathered to pray. It was at prayer that they found the strength not only to bear up under their imprisonment, but to discover a source of grace in their very tribulations. If there were priests among them, they celebrated Mass. If there were not, priests came from outside to celebrate with them. It even happened, on certain occasions, that Christians felt such a need to have someone to direct their prison community that they selected one of the presbyters among them to be consecrated as their bishop. (Bishops were selected by the communities themselves in the early days: Eusebius, *The Martyrs of Palestine,* chap. 7, p. 360.)

CHRISTIAN CONDUCT: WITNESS OF A WAY OF LIFE, CONFIDENCE IN VICTORY

What impresses us when we study the history of these first three centuries is the power of the witness borne by the confessors and martyrs. With firm step they strode off to trial, and answered the judges unhesitatingly in the name of their faith: "We are Christians." They knew what awaited them, but they did not flinch, as we see from the martyrdom of Saint Polycarp, for example:

The proconsul asked if he was Polycarp, and when he admitted it, he tried to persuade him to deny, saying: "Have regard for your age," and other things after these, which they are accustomed to say: "Swear by the genius of Caesar, repent, say: 'Away with the atheists.' " And when the governor pressed him and said: "Swear, and I shall release you: revile Christ," Polycarp said: "For eighty-six years have I served Him, and He has done me no wrong, and how can I blaspheme my King who saved me?" . . . And the proconsul said: "I have wild beasts; I shall throw you to them unless you repent." And he said: "Call them, for repentance from better to worse must not be made by us. . . ." And he again said to him: "I shall cause you to be consumed by fire, if you look down upon wild beasts, unless you repent." Polycarp said: "You threaten a fire that burns for a time and after a little is extinguished. . . ." And saying these and many other things, he was filled with courage and joy, and his face was suffused with grace, so that he did not fall, although disturbed by what was being said to him; on the other hand, the proconsul was amazed [Eusebius, *Ecclesiastical History,* book 4, chap. 15, pp. 238–39].

This was the general attitude of the confessors and martyrs—steadfast, sure of victory, ready for all consequences. The elderly—like Polycarp, bishop of Smyrna, and Potinus, ninety years of age, bishop of Lyons—as well as the young, women, and even children, faced death as if it were life, accepting their sentence in all serenity. There were individual martyrs, and there were groups of martyrs. A group could number as many as thirty, sixty, or a hundred persons.

A spirituality of martyrdom dominated the Christian awareness of the age. Many went to the tribunals of their own accord to declare their faith:

> For example, as soon as the decision was made against the first, one after another they jumped up to the tribunal before the judge, confessing themselves Christians, being completely unconcerned about the terrors and the various forms of torture, but speaking boldly without dismay about their religion for the God of the universe, and with joy and laughter and gladness accepting the last judgment of death, so that they sang and sent hymns and thanksgivings up to the God of the universe until the very last breath [ibid., book 8, chap. 9, p. 179].

The Christians who had not been denounced and were not in captivity attended the interrogations, tortures, and martyrdom of their sisters and brothers, along with other spectators of these public events, exhorting them to steadfastness in their sufferings, especially when they saw anyone in danger of weakening. On the latter occasions they would shout their words of support and encouragement at the risk of their own lives. Even soldiers in attendance, converts to Christianity, would encourage waverers in this way. Not infrequently, Christians would spontaneously declare themselves in order to be allowed to join their brothers and sisters in martyrdom and thus encourage and strengthen them.

Naturally, those who had families suffered from their separation from them, which supplied still another reason why they might be led to the point of yielding. While still an adolescent, Origen,

concerned that this might happen in the case of his father, wrote to
him on the eve of his (his father's) martyrdom: "Take care not to
weaken in your resolve for our sake"—for the sake of Origen and
his mother.

Even pagans admired the conduct of the Christians:

> A great and heroic deed this—and I know not what mystery
> reigns here, whereby he is broken neither by pain nor by such
> horrible tortures. . . . For I believe that he has children,
> indeed that his spouse and consort is in his house; and yet he
> neither yields to this love nor allows himself to be vanquished
> by compassion. This is a thing worthy of scrutiny—so deep a
> valor in the inmost depths of a person. This profession
> cannot be a frivolous thing—whatever else it might be—when
> an individual is capable of suffering for it and of refusing to
> withdraw in the face of death [*De laude martyrii,* 15, cited in
> *Actas de los mártires,* p. 159].

Women, too, bore outstanding witness. One of them was Am-
monarion:

> When the judge tortured her very vigorously for a long time,
> since she had declared beforehand that she would speak
> nothing of what he ordered, having made her promise true,
> [she] was led away. As for the rest, the most revered aged
> woman Mercuria, and she of many children, . . . Dionysia,
> when the governor became ashamed to carry on tortures to
> no avail and to be worsted by women, met death by the sword
> [Eusebius, *Ecclesiastical History,* book 6, chap. 41, p. 74].

A constant is discernible in the martyrs of diverse ages, sexes,
and conditions of life: fidelity above all else, above self-love, above
human relationships, above life itself. " 'What harm is it to say,
"Lord Caesar," and to offer sacrifice, and to be saved?' At first he
did not answer, but when they persisted, he said: 'I do not intend to
do what you advise me' " (ibid., book 4, chap. 15, p. 237).

For his part, Papylus's response was:

> I have served God from my youth and I have never offered
> sacrifice to idols. I am a Christian, and you cannot hear any

more from me than this; for there is nothing greater or nobler that I can say ["Acts of Carpus, Papylus, and Agathonicê," in *Acts of the Christian Martyrs, p. 27*].

Nor was age a handicap when it came to the steadfast Christian profession of faith:

> Hero and Ater and Isidore, Egyptians, and with them a youth of about fifteen years, Dioscorus, were delivered up. And at first when [the governor] tried to deceive the boy by words, as one easily led astray, and to force him by tortures, as one easily yielding, Dioscorus neither obeyed nor gave way. He very savagely tore the rest in pieces, and when they endured gave them also over to the fire. But, since he [the governor] admired Dioscorus, who was so brilliant in public and answered most wisely to his questions in private, he dismissed him, saying that he granted him a respite for repentance because of his youth. And now the most marvelous Dioscorus is with us, having remained for a longer contest and a more lasting conflict [Eusebius, *Ecclesiastical History,* book 6, chap. 41, pp. 74–75].

Subjected to interrogation under torture, the martyrs of Palestine refused even to give their names and addresses. One of them "was ordered by the governor, Urbanus, to be torn with iron claws, and afterwards his face was unrecognizable by reason of the abuse thus inflicted. Yet, asked who he was, from what province he came, and where he dwelt, he but confessed himself a 'servant of Christ' " (Eusebius, *The Martyrs of Palestine,* chap. 4, pp. 348–49).

"The judge, addressing himself to the leader of the group in particular, asked him the same question, and by way of response received the name of a prophet." So it went with all the rest. Their home town was Jerusalem, they would say (meaning the Heavenly Jerusalem). Then the judge would become very angry, and insist that they were lying, but the Christians would hold out, even with their arms being twisted behind their backs and their feet being crushed and torn by some strange machine (ibid., chap. 11, pp. 384-85).

Not to betray the names of others was still more crucial to these

Christians. This stands out in the interrogation of Cyprian. "I wish to know from you," the preconsul said, "who the presbyters are who reside in this city." "Your laws do well," replied Cyprian, "to forbid informing. And so I cannot tell you who they are or inform against them" ("Actas Proconsulares," in *Actas de los Mártires,* p. 245).

Even the authorities had to admire the phenomenon of Christian resistance. Pliny the Younger, in his letter cited above, reports to Trajan that, despite all efforts, "there is no getting those who actually are Christians to do as they are told" (quoted in *Actas de los Mártires,* p. 245). Sabinus, a high magistrate in the time of Maximinus Daia, records in a letter to the provincial governors that "with the passage of so long a time it has been established that they cannot be persuaded *in any way* to abandon such stubbornness" (Eusebius, *Ecclesiastical History,* chap. 9, p. 208).

It was this attitude that left the imperial authorities so frustrated. What was one to do with a group of individuals who had no fear of brute force—who refused to submit even under threat of the cruelest tortures, and death? A fine description by the pagan author Epictetus might be summarized as follows: What makes a mighty ruler so fearful? His guards, his weapons, his sentinels, of course—in a word, his military apparatus. Now, a young child will nevertheless approach his quarters without any fear. Why? Because a child is unaware of the danger. Similarly, anyone not afraid to die will have no fear of the tyrant. Such will be the case with a madman, for instance, who has no concern for his wealth, his body, or the wife and children he would leave behind. Well now, *Christians generally are of this frame of mind.* And so what tyrant, what guards, or what weapons will ever frighten them? (cited in *Actas de los Mártires,* pp. 153–54).

Eusebius says substantially the same thing, writing to the martyrs of the persecution of Maximinus Daia. "And these actions went well for him with all except with Christians, who, despising death, counted such tyranny on his part as nothing," and even under the most horrible tortures, "displayed their endurance in behalf of religion rather than give to idols the piety due to God" (*Ecclesiastical History,* book 8, chap. 14, p. 196).

Lactantius pronounces the following eulogy on Donatus, a Christian who suffered tortures nine times without yielding:

After this sort to lord it over the lords of the earth is triumph indeed! Now, by your valour were they conquered, when you set at defiance their flagitious edicts, and through steadfast faith and the fortitude of your soul, you *routed all the vain terrors of tyrannical authority* [*Of the Manner in Which the Persecutors Died,* chap. 16, p. 307].

LOVE, FREEDOM, FAITH, HOPE: SOURCES OF CHRISTIAN STRENGTH

Love

Many of the martyrs were physically weak, not to mention the women, the young, and the old among them. The Christian community of Lyons wrote to the other churches about the events of A.D. 177, when its bishop and innumerable other Christians were martyred. Their message includes their praise for Blandina, a slave:

And all the wrath of the mob and of the governor and of soldiers beyond all measure fell upon . . . Blandina, through whom Christ pointed out that the things among men which appear mean and obscure and contemptible with God are deemed worthy of great glory *because of the love for Him* shown in power and not boasted in appearance [Eusebius, *Ecclesiastical History,* book 5, chap. 1, p. 277, italics added].

The strength that raised these individuals above themselves, above their physical and psychic limitations, that rendered them strong though they were weak, was love.

By love, Christians were completely emptied of themselves, to be opened fully to God and others. No longer was it themselves who commanded their existence, but Christ. No longer were they attracted by fleeting joys. Now it was the good of others, whom they considered to be their brothers and sisters, that fed their gladness. Their joy was in seeing others happy. In the measure that they took leave of themselves, it was Christ and others who filled them. And this is why their own well-being was not their ultimate satisfaction.

On the other hand, seeing others in a painful situation caused them pain, and they were willing to undergo difficulties in order to help them. Their concern centered on the opposite pole, on the good of others, on correspondence to God's love. What had to be suffered in order to arrive at this objective was secondary and incidental. For them this was one of the rules of the game of human life, the game of love.

Suffering and death were not to be fled when the call of God or neighbor had been heard. Christians were ready for anything. It was not a matter of doing something for someone at as little expense as possible. Here the pole, the central concern, would still be oneself. This would mean that one still had something of oneself to defend—a little well-being to preserve, or at least physical health, one's home, one's familiar, cozy spot. This would still be gift by measure, gift with limits. By contrast, love was self-emptying that permitted God and others—for God's presence implied others (Matt. 25:31–46)—to fill the empty space. It was not a matter of knowing whether there would be difficulties, or of finding some way to escape the tortures and martyrdom. As their existence was totally orientated to the other, what Christians were bent on was responding to the call of others, the needs of others. It was no coincidence that it was Christians, in times of public calamities, such as plagues, who most generously went to the aid of others, who were least concerned with contagion, who, despite the danger, threw themselves into the task of burying the dead, whereas the attitude of the pagans was just the opposite (Eusebius, *Ecclesiastical History,* book 7, chap. 22, pp. 123–26).

Christians were so permeated with the presence of God that to deny the faith caused them more torment than would physical sufferings. To deny the faith would have been to deny the love of God, to deny one's Friend, one's Father, one's Brother, one's Liberator. It would have been to deny "my King who saved me" (Eusebius, ibid., book 4, chap. 15, p. 238). To bear witness to the faith was to bear witness not to a thing, but to *someone* with whom these persons intimately lived and who was the joy of their life, someone who fulfilled their existence.

This is the reason why Christians had no fear of suffering torture, or of the pain of being torn apart physically. It was not their survival that polarized their concern. *Someone* polarized it, and filled them with strength. It was out of loyalty to Christ that they suffered all this. They did not do it as an obligation, a duty, but as an act of love, an act of friendship. This alone they would cherish and develop, and never breach. "Christ suffering in [the martyr Sanctus] manifested great glory, routing his Adversary and for the example of the rest showing that there is *nothing to be feared where there is love of the Father* and nothing painful where there is Christ's glory" (Eusebius, ibid., book 5, chap. 1, p. 278, italics added). "They did not give up their resolution, *'because perfect charity casteth out fear'* [1 John 4:18]" (Letter of the imprisoned Bishop Phileas to his flock, ibid., book 8, chap. 10, p. 181, italics added).

Evangelical poverty was understood first and foremost as detachment from oneself in order to be filled with the presence of God and others. This is why Christians were unattached to things, seeing in them only the means of service to others (Matt. 19:27). They refused to be guided by attachment to their families, when loyalty to Christ demanded the supreme witness. They were able to take leave of those dear to them to achieve a greater good (Matt. 19:29). There was *someone* among them who took the place of all these other goods, and revitalized them. The focus of their lives was outside these things. Their personal fulfillment was the fulfillment of their sisters and brothers, and the fulfillment of their elder brother, Christ. This is the reason why they were able to suffer hunger, thirst, imprisonment, and torment—because for them, real value did not reside in food and drink and comfort, those pagan concerns from which they held themselves apart (Luke 12:22–34). It was another ideal that attracted them and satisfied them. Nor was it a random ideal: it was *someone,* someone who fulfilled all their longings for intense life, for encounter, for human depth, for happiness, for love.

The confidence the Christians placed in God was absolute. They trusted that, in the hour of their interrogation, the Spirit would speak for them (Matt. 10:20), and would give them the strength to bear up under their trials. Instead of trusting in their own abilities, Christians trusted in the power of God (2 Cor. 12:9–10). Prayer, then, individual as well as in community, occupied a most important place in their lives. A personal relationship with Christ was fundamental. Whether in the community liturgy or in the intimacy of personal prayer, Christians developed a love relationship with God, fed on God, received from God the strength for total self-gift, for surrender without limit. It was God whom they sought, who was the infinite that filled them, who was happiness that could grow even in the most horrible situations.

Freedom

Christians had a clear awareness that their clinging to Christ was more important than anything else—that staying strong was staying free, whereas yielding meant becoming slaves of might, of tyranny. In order to be free, the Christian had to be willing to lose physically freedom and life itself. After all, true liberty, true life, was manifested in its highest degree in "confession," and in martyrdom. In the year 202, Saints Perpetua, Felicity, Satyrus, and three others—five catechumens and their catechist—were sentenced at Carthage. As they were being led into the arena, there was an attempt on the part of their captors to force them to don pagan garments. But they responded, "We came to this of our own free will, that *our freedom should not be violated"* ("Acts of Perpetua and Felicitas," chap. 18, in *Acts of the Christian Martyrs,* p. 127, italics added). Bishop Phileas recounts:

> The remainder [having suffered torments and been returned to their cells], obtaining recovery under treatment *with time and by their stay in prison, became more confident.* Thus, then, when the choice lay before them and the order was given either to touch the abominable sacrifice and be undisturbed, receiving from them the *accursed freedom,* or not to sacrifice and to receive the death penalty, without hesitation they gladly went to their death [Eusebius, *Ecclesiastical History,* book 8, chap. 10, p. 183, italics added].

Under Urbanus, governor of Palestine, a certain "Dominus, very well known to all in Palestine for his *extraordinary boldness,"* his extraordinary freedom, was consigned to the flames because of his constancy in enduring previous torments (Eusebius, *The Martyrs of Palestine,* chap. 7, p. 361, italics added).

Freedom or boldness meant the courage to be what one was—a disciple of Christ—to proclaim the truth, and to follow one's faith without regard for the threats of tyrannical might. In order to be free, Christians had no fear of losing their external liberty—their freedom of movement, even their freedom of life. To be sure, this was a radical option, and judges always chanted the paeans of liberty in order to soften the determination of Christians. The martyr Agapius was "asked with a promise of liberty to renounce his resolve." But he remained strong (Eusebius, ibid., chap. 6, p. 357). The martyr Eubulus "was long entreated by the judge to offer sacrifice and so enjoy the liberty they think they can give. But he preferred a glorious death for religion to this transitory life" (ibid., chap. 11, p. 394).

Faith

"Another girl, in body mean, but strong in soul, and possessed of a great mind which gave *strength to the meanness of her body"* and so outraged at the inhumanity being practiced upon a fellow Christian of hers, cried from the midst of the crowd, "And how long dost thou torture my sister so cruelly?" At once she was dragged from the multitude and carried off to be tortured (Eusebius, *Martyrs of Palestine,* chap. 8, pp. 367–68, italics added).

It is instructive to observe the extent to which a Christian's admirable behavior under torture, in prison, and in martyrdom, was not a matter of the physical, but of determination. What counted was firmness in faith, hope in God, and a love that persuaded you to give up your life for your sisters and brothers. And surely enough, when persecution flared up once more, after some respite, "again the divine power of our Savior inspired its champions with such courage that they *needed neither inducement nor urging* to spurn the threats of these mighty persons (ibid., chap. 9, p. 372, italics added).

Of course, training for confession and martyrdom was not physical. It was the Christian life, daily and intense. It was the depth and interiority of this life—the capacity for self-renouncement, humility, detachment from earthly goods, service, and vital self-donation in the everyday life. The great majority of Christians were of humble origin. Their experience of a difficult life, where privation and suffering were scarcely lacking, was also an influential factor:

> Such, then, was the diversity in age to be found among them. On the other hand, they varied in mental development. Some still had the uninstructed and simple mind of a child, others were altogether of a sturdy and weighty character, and among their number were men by no means ignorant of sacred learning. But in all was to be found, as a natural quality, *bravery of a surpassing and valiant order* [Eusebius, ibid., chap. 11, p. 379, italics added].

Hope

One thing impressed the pagans more than anything else—the contempt Christians had for death. Justin tells us of his conversion:

> I heard the Christians being abused, but seeing them fearless in the face of death and of all things thought frightful, I concluded that it was impossible for them to exist in wickedness and libertinism [Eusebius, *Ecclesiastical History,* book 4, chap. 8, p. 220].

There was a very deep eschatological awareness in Christians. Hope was a virtue intensely lived, and not merely individually, but collectively. Hope in a world to come, in a new heaven and a new earth, which had already begun with Christ's resurrection, was their hallmark. Christians carried within them this certainty of the new life inaugurated by the Lord who had been raised from the dead. Despite the opacity of faith, hope was their greatest guarantee that in suffering and death, love had begun its final conquest of hate.

After hearing his death sentence, an African martyr of the year 180 said, "Today we are martyrs in heaven. Thanks be to God!" ("Acts of the Scillitan Martyrs," chap. 6, in *Acts of the Christian Martyrs,* p. 89). The spirituality of martyrdom was intimately connected with the certitude of resurrection. Even the pagans were obliged to take cognizance of this fact. "The poor wretches have convinced themselves, first and foremost, that they are going to be immortal and live for all time, in consequence of which they despise death and even willingly give themselves into custody, most of them" (Lucian, *The Passing of Peregrinus,* no. 13, p. 15). The pagans held that bodies left without burial could not rise, which was why they so often prevented Christians from burying the bodies of their martyrs. The corpses were left in the open air, or cremated by the pagans themselves: in reducing them to ashes, they sought to deprive Christians of their hope of resurrection, to "deprive them of the rebirth, in order, as they said, 'that they might not even have hope of resurrection, by trusting in which they introduced among us a strange and new religion and, despite terrors, going readily and joyfully to death . . .' " (Eusebius, *Ecclesiastical History,* book 5, chap. 1, ad fin.).

APOSTASY

> Some of the seed landed on rocky ground where it had little soil [Mark 4:5].

We have already seen that alongside the striking witness of martyrs and confessors, there were innumerable instances of defeat, fear, retreat, and betrayal.

There were three kinds of apostates: the *sacrificati,* those who had taken part in sacrifice to the gods; the *thurificati,* who had only offered a few grains of incense to the honor of the emperor; and the *libellatici,* who had not offered sacrifice, but had in one way or another obtained the *libellus,* the certificate, to the effect that they had indeed done so, which exempted them from persecution and repression. Christians considered all three types of apostasy as gravely sinful and the equivalent of self-excommunication. Anyone doing such a thing denied Christ.

There were likewise three degrees of betrayal: there were those who, immediately upon hearing of the edict of persecution, made for the altars to offer sacrifice and escape tribulation; then there were those who had yielded after being arrested and having spent a number of days in prison; and finally there were those who fell only upon having been tortured. It was also considered seriously wrong by Christians to have complied with other determinations of the edicts, such as, for example, to have delivered up sacred books—

traditio—or to have reported the names and addresses of other Christians.

The presbyters, the elders, of Rome wrote concerning Christians of that city during the persecution of Decius:

> The Church stands firmly in faith although some, compelled by the very terror itself, whether because they were distinguished persons or seized with the fear of men, have fallen [Cyprian, *Letters,* 8, p. 22].

Among the fallen were many who had bought immunity at the price of gold. The rich, especially, chose to preserve their goods and honors. The vacillation of some had an influence on the morale of the less than stout, contributing to their ambiguous comportment.

Denis, bishop of Alexandria, in a letter to Fabius, bishop of Antioch, paints the following picture:

> Many of the more eminent came forward immediately in some instances through fear; others who held public positions were forced to do so by their official duties; still others were drawn on by those about them. [Some did so with great regret,] . . . but some others ran to the altars more boldly, maintaining stoutly by their boldness that they had never been Christians even formerly, and concerning these the Lord's prediction is most true that they shall "hardly" be saved [Eusebius, *Ecclesiastical History,* book 6, chap. 41].

After all, "only with difficulty will a rich man enter into the kingdom of God" (Matt. 19:23). The *Shepherd of Hermas,* an important early Christian work dating from the end of the first century, compares the rich, and persons weighed down with the cares of the world, to a mountian covered with thorns. They are unsuitable for the church because they are attached to the goods of this world. When persecution comes upon them, their wealth leads them to deny Christ (*Shepherd of Hermas,* similitude 9, vision 3).

To be sure, there were highly placed persons whose conduct under torture was most admirable. But the Roman presbyters Denis, Hermas, and Cyprian, too, make the same observation: among those who yielded, there was a higher proportion of wealthy persons—or, better, attachment to wealth was the major cause of betrayal. These persons' zeal for material goods, their bonds with the things of the world, weighed them down, made them insensitive, rendered them incapable of greater deeds and love of others, incapable of union with Christ as manifested in steadfastness under torture and the witness of martyrdom. These deeds demanded profound liberty, an acute sensitivity vis-à-vis one's brothers and sisters, and a forthright renunciation of all that was of secondary import. After all, they were "not lords as regards their money but rather the bond-slaves of their money." Indeed, "how can they follow Christ who are held back by the chain of their personal property?" What they prize above all things is their own property rather than God, and this is a grave mistake (Cyprian, *The Lapsed,* chaps. 11–12, pp. 66–68).

Eusebius with his testimony of the persecution of Diocletian, and Cyprian with his of Decius's, made this same critical analysis, broadening their observations to include the whole church. Both persecutions occurred after long periods of tolerance, and the number of traitors was great. "When, because of greater freedom, our affairs went over to conceit and sloth," there were sterile discussions, intrigues, envy, and hypocrisy. Relaxation went so far as to include countenancing assumption by the laity of certain public tasks previously considered forbidden by reason of their intimate connection with paganism. Many bishops were concerned only with power (Eusebius, *Ecclesiastical History,* book 8, chap. 1, p. 165).

Cyprian attempts an analysis of the causes of so many apostasies. "We must not . . . dissimulate the truth, nor hush the occasion and cause of our sore," he says. The persecution was a trial, a test, a challenge permitted by the Lord by reason of the negligence into which the church had fallen in its behavior. "He wished to arouse faith, which had fallen weak, and as it were asleep." The reason for so many downfalls was the previous comportment of the church. Christians had been preoccupied with wealth, profit, and the amassing of possessions. They had given themselves over to pride, forgetting simplicity and loyalty. Their renunciation of material goods had become a matter of words rather than of deeds, with each one seeking to be ever up-to-date and "in style," doing their own thing without any regard for others. "Many bishops, who ought to be a source of encouragement and an example to the rest, contemning their divine charge came under the charge of secular kings" (Saint Cyprian, *The Lapsed,* chap. 6, p. 61).

It was natural, in such conditions, that the greater number of Christians would be unprepared for so difficult a combat as that of persecution. But the number of lapses served to make the church aware of what had happened and stir it from its slumber. The church had strayed from the route mapped out for it by its founder, whose role had been that of a poor servant. And surely enough, in Valerian's persecution, which followed upon those of Decius and Gallus, the attitude of Christians became generally more solid. Furthermore, one should not generalize from what occurred in the persecutions of Decius and Diocletian in particular, in a context of the third century and the beginning of the fourth, with their large number of apostasies and unworthy attitude on the part of the majority of the bishops, to the overall Christian experience of the first three centuries.

CHAPTER 3

A Theology of Persecution:
A Church Dynamized by the Spirit

THE CHURCH AND POWER: TWO SOLUTIONS

The persecutions occasioned great perplexity among Christians. Why were they being persecuted? They had done no evil, had committed no crime. To boot, they were accused of numberless aberrations in the practice of their "illicit superstition." It was all too paradoxical, and the apologists sprang up, early in the second century, to dissipate the calumnies and prejudices of the pagans, to be sure, but principally to demonstrate to public opinion the true nature of Christianity.

The apologists' concern was to show Christianity's conformity to the Hellenic ideal. For the apologists, the former was the full realization of the latter. Christians were the authentic heirs of Greco-Roman civilization. They were the finest citizens of the empire. The apologists not only appealed for tolerance, they proclaimed the alliance of Christianity and philosophy, church and empire. They accepted the world they lived in. The *Letter to Diognetus* insisted that Christians were no different from other citizens, either in domicile, dress, or language. Justin presented the Christian virtues, placing the accent on obedience to law. Melito of Sardis stated that there could scarcely be anything to militate against a complete *entente* between church and empire—the very syncronicity of their appearance in the world (the empire had been founded only some thirty years before Christ) seemed to presage the destiny of both to the same grandeur.

But the apologists had a bone to pick with the empire, too, and it was a matter of the first importance. The empire persecuted Christians. The apologists tried to show (as did other, later Christian writers, such as Lactantius and Eusebius) that the emperors who had persecuted Christians were bad emperors—that they were incompetent, depraved, violent exploiters—whereas the others had been good emperors. The truth was often just the contrary, but the apologists seemed not to notice (Daniélou and Marrou, *First Six Hundred Years,* pp. 90–93).

Then a very different tendency appeared among Christian writers, especially Origen, Tertullian, and Hippolytus. After the apologists, the accent was suddenly on apocalyptic expectations, a restless Judeo-Christian messianism centered upon the imminent return of Christ and hence on integral asceticism.

Tertullian was the partisan of a Christianity of combat, which would confront the pagan world head-on and accept no relationship with it. He was faithful to the sort of apocalyptic Christianity that set church and empire in radical opposition, "brooking no conciliation, either with the Caesars, or with the traditions of Rome, or with the prejudices of the aristocracy," and thus striking no compromise whatever. He criticized pagan culture, customs, and values en bloc. He forbade Christian participation in collective demonstrations, criticized those who were concerned with being in the latest style, attempted to demonstrate the incompatibility of the faith with numerous other credal professions, and counseled conscientious objection.

In their eschatology of urgency, their mighty hope in the imminence of the parousia, Origen, Tertullian, and Hippolytus all showed the same indifference to the fate of the city of earth. What they hoped for from it was martyrdom, which would manifest its incompatibility with the city of God. The Joannine writers, including the author of Revelation, fomented their image of the tension between the imperial power and the church. Their criticism of the empire, accordingly, was directed not only against the persecutions but against the imperial authority itself.

Hippolytus waged a crucial polemic with Pope Callistus. There were doctrinal points on which he found himself at odds with the bishop of Rome, but, further, he censured him for his concern for good relations with the imperial power, and for letting himself be led to a certain leniency toward it. The milieu falling principally under Hippolytus's guns was that of Christians of the ruling classes, whose situation was politically delicate, and who had a horror of attitudes that might provoke the sleeping giant and unleash a new persecution. And this was the social matrix that produced most of the leaders of the church. The church was interested in keeping in the good graces of the ruling caste, which could be of great assistance to it in avoiding friction and obviating difficulties. For Hippolytus, the church should be poor, without possessions, and in permanent conflict with the world. Persecution is the normal situation. Coexistence is not to be sought, indeed is impossible. The ideal for every Christian is martyrdom (Daniélou and Marrou, *First Six Hundred Years,* pp. 152–71).

Meanwhile, with respect to the *lapsi,* those who had fallen, Novatian appeared on the scene as the leader of a group of rigorists who accepted no reconciliation with them whatever. Once fallen, they had no hope of forgiveness. The position of the church generally was not this extreme. On the contrary, the church reacted against this current.

In the following pages I shall examine the position of the majority of the bishops with respect to a series of problems raised by persecution. In chapters 1 and 2 we have seen the practice of the church; now we shall investigate its principles—the theory, or theology, orientating Christian activity in persecution, martyrdom, imprisonment, hiding, flight, apostasy, and penance.

BLESSED ARE THE PERSECUTED

In the theological writings of the age, there is a clear awareness, rooted in experience and in the gospel, that persecution of Christians is not an abnormality. "No wonder we suffer constant persecution, and are momentarily assaulted by painful tribulation, for the Lord has foretold that this must occur" (Cyprian, "Preparation for Martyrdom," cited in *Actas de los Mártires,* pp. 673–85). Persecution was good fortune and happiness, a nonpareil opportunity to testify to faith and hope, a wellspring of the highest examples of generosity, devotion, love, and freedom. "The Lord has willed that we rejoice and exult in it. This is the path that the Lord himself has followed for the deliverance of all. What he has instructed us to do, this he has done before us, and what he has exhorted us to suffer, he has first suffered for us" (ibid.).

Persecution is a combat, more sublime than any other. "If we have placed ourselves in Christ's service, we cannot think only of peace, and refuse the combat, for the first to throw himself into the struggle was the Lord" (ibid.). Confrontation is inevitable:

> If the world persecutes us with its hate, Christ bore the hate of the world before us. If we must bear insults, flight, torture in this world, let us remember that the Creator and Lord of the world had to bear them before us, and that he gave us fair warning, saying, "The hour is coming when everyone who kills you will think that he is rendering service to God" [ibid.].

From the foundation of the world, justice suffers persecution. "It has been ordained from the beginning of the world that this same justice should struggle in the worldly conflict, since, immediately in the very beginning, Abel the just was killed and thenceforth all the just men and prophets and the apostles who were sent forth" (Cyprian, *Letters,* 6, no. 2, p. 17).

The Christian is not to be naive:

> Let us not imagine that what is to come will be easy. The struggle that threatens will be hard and fierce, and soldiers of Christ must prepare themselves for it with incorruptible faith and unshakable firmness. If we daily drink the cup of the blood of Christ, it is in order to be ready to shed our blood for Christ as well [ibid.].

The condition for such readiness will be the following of Christ, who lives and who transmits life, and breach with a dying world, detachment from material satisfaction, or a stable situation, or pagan values:

> God has willed, beloved brethren, that there be none among you who in any way would flag in the face of persecution,

being armed beforehand with the words of the gospel, and ready for anything that might happen [ibid.].

The enemy is at hand. Our position must be strong. We must not fear those who can but destroy the body, and then nothing else. Death, for a Christian, is not a destruction but a coronation: " 'We suffer with him that we may also be glorified with him' [Rom. 8:17]" (ibid., p. 18). " 'Who loves life loses it, and who loses his life for my love keeps it for life eternal' [John 12:25]" (ibid.). This is the consciousness of the primitive church. Persecution forms the backdrop of all Christian reflection. To speak of the Christian life without referring to persecution is impossible. It is viewed less as an evil than as an opportunity for witness, and for a deepening of the life of faith. It is also a challenge, by which faith is tested, refined, and made perfect, or instead, demonstrated not to have deep roots. "The faithful were few, then, but faithful they were, walking in the narrow, open way that leads to life" (ibid.).

Christians had attached themselves to a person, Jesus Christ. They were committed to a community, opting for a new kind of life that involved a radical rupture with their former, thoroughly pagan, life. To love the sisters and brothers through concrete acts, to proclaim one's faith even at the risk of one's life, were basic exigencies for every Christian. The same radicality of life was demanded of the catechumen as of the bishop, and no difference of age, sex, or community function was deemed important. There was diversity of function and charism in the church, but the living of the radicality of the gospel was a demand upon *all,* without distinction. All were expected to be ready to give a living account of their hope, to confess the faith when interrogated. There was to be no shilly-shallying. There was to be no shadow of doubt, no hesitation:

Let us stand fast lest there arise in us any hesitation whether we should deny or confess, lest Elijah's word be also said to us, "How long will you go on limping on both your thighs? If the Lord is God, follow him (1 Kings 18:21)" [Origen, *Exhortation to Martyrdom,* no. 18, p. 55].

Cyprian, in his treatise *De Lapsis* ("on those who have lapsed"), holds that the very thought of sacrificing, or of obtaining a certificate, calls for an act of repentance. "If anyone in this faithless and corrupt age is ashamed of me and my doctrine, the Son of Man will be ashamed of him" (Mark 8:38), Cyprian reminds us. How can you consider yourself a Christian when you are ashamed or afraid to be a Christian? How can you be with Christ if you fear, and feel it to be dishonorable, to belong to Christ? (chap. 28).

The following text of Origen is a precious vignette of the Christian thinking of the age:

> For even in our day, our Lord and Savior Jesus Christ, prince of our militia, cries to those who soldier with him: "Let the one who is fearful and of little courage not come to my wars!" And this, indeed, in different words, but with the same meaning, is what the gospel says: "Who does not take up the cross and follow me is not worthy of me," and "Who does not hate father and mother and brothers and sisters and life itself cannot be my disciple." And again "Who does not renounce all possessions cannot be my disciple" (cf. Luke 14:26–33). Is it not evident that, by these words, Christ expels from his camps all of the timid and cowardly? Thus, then, all of you who desire to belong to Christ's militia, and remain in its encampments, keep all fear of soul far from you. . . . Would you learn how all of this is easy for those who enter the combat with faith? In these encampments, even women win, for it is not by stoutness of body that one struggles here, but by the strength of one's faith. . . . Those who do battle for truth, who war for God, have need not of strength of body, but of soul, for it is not with weapons of iron that the victory is gained, but with prayer. It is faith that provides stamina in the combat [Origen, *Homily 9 on the Book of Judges,* no. 1; in *Actas de los Mártires,* pp. 55–56].

Or, as Tertullian put it: "The flesh is weak and the spirit is ready. Let flesh fear the torments as it may; if the spirit is ready, the flesh will endure with serenity" (*Exhortation to the Martyrs,* no. 4; in *Actas de los Mártires,* p. 389).

Martyrdom

> Unless the grain of wheat falls to the earth and dies . . . [John 12:24].

A basic prerequisite for Christian witness is renunciation. "The world has been crucified to me and I to the world" (Gal. 6:14; see Clement of Alexandria, *Stromata,* book 2, chap. 20 [in *Actas de los Mártires,* p. 38]). One must bear insults, ridicule, sarcasm of every sort, and physical sufferings in the bargain. But this is impossible "when we are drawn by our affection for our children or for their mother or for any of those we hold dearest in life to hold onto them and to stay alive." No, we must "belong totally to God and to life with Him and near Him, as those who will join in communion with His Only Begotten Son and His fellows (cf. Heb. 3:14)" (Origen, *Exhortation to Martyrdom,* no. 11, p. 48). In the measure of our detachment from all these goods—something in which the Christian undergoes daily training—conditions are present for a victorious confrontation with the uncertainty and spoliation of persecution:

> The more familiar we are with poverty, with a lack of ease, with privations, the readier we are for battle. Only renunciation makes for the freedom one needs to stand firm in the Lord. All else is encumbrance, and the likely occasion of a fall [Cyprian, *De Lapsis,* in *Actas de los Mártires,* pp. 572–73].

A spirituality of martyrdom dominated the theory and practice of the primitive Christian communities. To die for the faith was not seen as a defeat, but as the victory of those whom violence had been unable to bend. To die for the faith was seen as the supreme exercise of freedom, for martyrs had refused, despite all the pressures, to deviate from their option:

> For what more glorious or more felicitous could happen to any man from the divine condescension than, undaunted before the very executioners, to confess the Lord God; than to confess Christ, the Son of God, among the various and refined tortures of the cruel secular power and even with the body twisted and racked and butchered and even dying yet with a *free spirit* . . . than to receive the heavenly kingdom without any delay; than to have been made a colleague in the Passion with Christ; than to have been made a *judge of one's*

judge by the divine condescension . . . than not to have obeyed human and sacrilegious laws against faith . . . than, by dying, to have overcome death itself which is feared by all . . . than to have struggled against all of the pains of a mutilated body with strength of spirit . . . than to account it life that one has lost one's own? . . .

And we have conquered the enemies of God already by this very fact that we have not yielded. And we have overcome nefarious laws against truth [letter of the presbyters Moses, Maximus, and their companions, from prison, in Cyprian, *Letters,* 31, nos. 3, 5, pp. 80–82, italics added].

The same notion of the dignity of persecution in the cause of justice, the same awareness of the freedom that is made manifest in fortitude, is to be found in Cyprian when he speaks of professing one's faith:

With his body placed in chains, [Celerinus's] spirit remained *released and free.* . . . He lay among [his] tortures stronger than his torturers; confined, greater than those who confined him; prostrate, loftier than those who stand; bound, firmer than those who bound; judged, more sublime than those who judge [ibid., 39, no. 2, pp. 99–100, italics added].

The glory of "confession" is no less than that of martyrdom:

The longer your fight, the more sublime your crown! The one struggle is but the heaping up of a manifold number of battles. With the firmness of an oak, you conquer hunger and you despise thirst and you tread underfoot the squalor of the prison and the horror of the penal cell.

Punishment is overcome there; torture is crushed. Death . . . is conquered by the reward of immortality [ibid., 37, no. 3, p. 96].

"You confess as often as you are asked to come out of prison [through an act of betrayal] and prefer the prison with faith and courage," says Cyprian (ibid., no. 1, p. 94).

"The Word of God Is Not Chained"

The Christian view of imprisonment was basically positive. Not that Christians saw imprisonment as an ideal to be striven for—they recognized the evil that it represented. However, by reason of the privations it involved, imprisonment favored a growth, a deepening of the Christian life, in a way not to be found elsewhere. No one emerged from prison without being profoundly marked by the experience. "Prison is for the Christian what the wilderness is for the prophet" (Tertullian, *Exhortation to the Martyrs,* in *Actas de los Mártires,* pp. 384–93): a place of spiritual apprenticeship.

Deprived of material goods and comforts, having to bear the stench, the promiscuity, the unspeakably bad food, the cold, hunger, thirst, isolation, the dark, fetters, and all of the rest, Christians in prison had to discover their source of life, gladness, and communion within themselves. This source was *faith.* In the absence of all material or sensible support and comfort, faith became stronger, firmer. Christians were no longer dissipated by the innumerable compensations of the life of the free. They were led to delve for the essential, they had to find the raison d'être of their lives, their struggle, their hope, in God alone. "Let us call prison a 'retreat,' " they said (ibid.). Now they came to appreciate true freedom, a freedom independent of walls and iron bars, a liberty within them. It was their decision whether to lose it or develop it.

This freedom created among Christians in prison an atmosphere that was free of the restrictions of walls and gratings. They themselves, and not the material edifice surrounding them, determined the quality of their lives. "The jail is dark, but *you are light.* It is full of chains, but *you are free for God.* A judge is on the way, but *you shall be judging the judges"* (ibid., italics added).

Numberless passages from the Christian writers of the era call the confessors and martyrs "athletes of faith," referring to the passage from Saint Paul about those who run a race in a stadium: "Athletes deprive themselves of all sorts of things. They do this to win a crown of leaves that withers, but we a crown that is imperishable" (1 Cor. 9:25). The Christian life is an ongoing confrontation, for which one must be prepared. Prison is wicked, but it provides training, exercise. "Virtue, you see, is built through fitness, and

destroyed through softness" (Tertullian, *Exhortation,* ibid.).
Imprisonment, then, is a genuine grace. It is a desert, a retreat, a training for the encounter with God and with all men and women (see ibid.).

As we have noted, many Christians were banished, sentenced to exile. Cyprian wrote some letters concerning these confessors, for a number of them who had behaved admirably during their interrogations had failed to match this heroic conduct after their release. Several aspects of their comportment were open to criticism. There were even some who gloried in their heroic conduct, boasting of the past but failing to bear witness in the present. Cyprian cited the duty of others, in fellowship, to reprehend, correct, and upbraid them. He laid great emphasis on community life, pointing out that there should be no quarrels, misunderstandings, or rivalries among them.

Tertullian, writing to his brothers and sisters in captivity, likewise insists on this point: Christians look to the confessors for peace and concord, which is an additional reason for them to be fully united with the community in one heart and one soul (*Exhortation to the Martyrs,* chap. 1; in *Actas de los Mártires,* p. 385). Cyprian concludes with an exhortation to the effect that it is not enough to confess Christ before the authorities; one must live the faith not only in prison and in exile, but throughout one's life:

> We are still in the world, still drawn up in line of battle; we fight daily for our lives. . . . You have been made an example to the rest of the brethren for whose living your life and actions ought to be a stimulation [Cyprian, *Letters,* 13, no. 2, p. 37].

SAFETY AND FLIGHT: CHRISTIAN WISDOM AND FEARLESSNESS

Certain problems especially came under discussion in the age of the persecutions. One was that of spontaneous surrender, flight, and the norms for self-protection. Clement, bishop of Alexandria, sums up the majority position in the church:

When [the Lord] says, "When they persecute you in this city, flee ye to the other [Matt. 10:23]," He does not advise flight, as if persecution were an evil thing; nor does He enjoin them by flight to avoid death, as if in dread of it, but wishes us neither to be the authors nor abettors of any evil to any one, either to ourselves or the persecutor and murderer. For He, in a way, bids us take care of ourselves. But he who disobeys is rash and foolhardy. If he who kills a man of God sins against God, he also who presents himself before the judgment-seat becomes guilty of his death. And such is also the case with him who does not avoid persecution, but out of daring presents himself for capture. Such a one, as far as in him lies, becomes an accomplice in the crime of the persecutor. And if he also uses provocation, he is wholly guilty, challenging the wild beast [Clement of Alexandria, *Stromata,* book 4, chap. 10, p. 423].

There would seem to have been a great many instances when, from a distorted view of martyrdom, Christians would decide that once a persecution was in progress the ideal was to be murdered by the persecutors. And so they would courageously make for the tribunals and present themselves as Christians, in order to receive the "crown of martyrdom." Clement sternly scores this conduct, labeling it complicity. These Christians are collaborating with the persecutors. The ideal was not to die, but to live in Christ. Those who were arrested ought to be up to sacrificing their lives in defense of their option. Here, death had its full meaning as a testimonial to freedom, steadfastness of faith, and love for one's sisters and brothers. This was not death actually brought on oneself. This was death dealt by the persecutors because the Christian refused to turn traitor. This is Cyprian's position, too, and that of the great majority of the bishops. "Our principles prohibit our surrendering spontaneously" ("Respuesta al interrogatório judicial," in *Actas de los Mártires,* p. 757).

One reason for this policy was to preclude betrayal that might occur as a result of poor preparation. Inevitably those most in haste to be made martyrs were insufficiently mature to confront the pressure of the suffering involved, and ended by retreating when they were still short of the goal. This was the reproach made by the church of Smyrna with regard to a man who had spontaneously surrendered and then had yielded, so that he "too hastily, but not with a religious spirit, had rushed to the tribunal with others, and so, when convicted, gave clear proof to all that such men should not become daring recklessly and without a religious spirit" (Eusebius, *Ecclesiastical History,* book 4, chap. 15, p. 235).

In the text cited earlier, Clement reproves such provocation as indicative of an immature attitude. Christians will not abandon their faith simply because it disturbs the oppressor, to be sure; but neither ought they to add further provocation (such as by spontaneous self-denunciation), for this only occasions repression. It leaves the oppressor without freedom to behave otherwise. And so Christians ought not to expose themselves to danger. They should take concrete measures to escape arrest. They ought to follow certain norms of safety, lest they themselves provide the framework for their persecutors' cruel acts. Thus when persecution broke out in Smyrna or Carthage, bishops Polycarp and Cyprian went into hiding, in homes that would not be visited by soldiers. Twice we find them in places of refuge outside the city. The community took responsibility for providing places where those highest on the "wanted list" could hide. Polycarp moves from one location to another. Cyprian, from his place of refuge, follows the course of events, and continues to direct his community. It is from here that he provides his flock with certain norms for protecting themselves:

> Although the brethren in their love are desirous of coming together and visiting the good confessors . . . yet I think that this ought to be done cautiously and not in crowds and not through a multitude united together at a single time, lest from that very fact hatred be stirred up and permission for entering be refused and while, insatiable, we wish much, we lose all. Take heed, therefore, and provide that this may be done more safely with moderation so that the priests also who offer Sacrifice there among the confessors may alternate one by one, by turns, with one deacon for each, since a change of persons and an alternation of those assembling lessens ill will [Cyprian, *Letters,* 5, no. 2, p. 15].

Another norm followed was to avoid community assemblies in open or public places. Depending on circumstances, groups could either be small or could gather in some secure location. As we have seen, the catacombs were used.

The question of flight provoked extensive discussion. Some, like Tertullian, were entirely opposed to it. No one, they thought, ought to evade the opportunity of martyrdom, and they spoke out against any norms of security. The majority, however, including Origen, considered flight to be a correct procedure. In fact, flight was actually a type of confession, perhaps indeed a kind of martyrdom. After all, it implied a very serious attitude of renunciation and self-deprivation. Generally Christians would have to abandon all their goods, and hazard a life that could be as difficult as prison itself.

Denis, bishop of Alexandria, refers in one of his letters to "the multitude of those who wandered in deserts and mountains, and who perished from hunger and thirst and frost and diseases and robbers and wild beasts" or were enslaved by barbaric tribes (Eusebius, *Ecclesiastical History,* book 6, chap. 42, p. 76). The fugitive was one who had chosen a life of insecurity. In his *De Lapsis,* Cyprian reprehends those who, in his opinion, ought to have fled but who were overattached to their material goods, and ended by being arrested and denying the faith (book 10, pp. 65-66).

In certain circumstances, then, flight was actually a matter of duty. This is Clement's position, as we have seen: flight is not recommended as if to be persecuted were an evil. Nor is it to be undertaken out of fear of death—no one who believes that resurrection springs from death on a cross can fear death. Flight is to be undertaken in order that the persecutor not perform a murderous act. A Christian's duty is to present obstacles to that act, by avoiding arrest—hence, at times, to run away. Of course, the Christian is ready for anything:

> The first title to victory is for him who has fallen in the hands of the Gentiles to confess the Lord; the second step to glory is to make a cautious withdrawal and then to keep himself for God. The one is a public confession; the other private. The former conquers the judge of the world; the latter satisfied with God as his judge guards a conscience pure by integrity of heart. In the former case fortitude is quicker; in the latter

solicitude is more secure. The one, as his hour approached, was then found ready; the other perhaps was delayed because he had left his estate and had withdrawn, for he would not deny; surely he would have confessed, had he also been seized [Saint Cyprian, *The Lapsed,* chap. 3, p. 59].

At all events, then, withdrawal is only intended as temporary: arrest and imprisonment may come later—and then the Christian will be prepared to give witness. Indeed, this is precisely what occurred in the case of Cyprian. In the persecution of Decius (A.D. 250–51), he withdrew, the better to guide his community. Six years later (A.D. 257) he was arrested and martyred, in the persecution under Valerian.

PENANCE: THE NEW PERSON VANQUISHES THE OLD

The question of poor conduct was one of the most urgent and most discussed problems with which Christians had to deal. The denial of the faith—under whatever conditions (prison, torture, and so on)—and the means of doing so (verbal or material, by sacrifice, incense, or certification) were considered a most grave sin. There was even question of whether it could be forgiven.

Here there were two extremes: the rigorists simply accepted no reconciliation with those who had weakened; the laxists considered that all of them should be reconciled without any ado. The position of the majority, however, was that degrees of misconduct should be distinguished, and that all the lapsed who were reconciled ought to have to submit to a lengthy period of penance. Penance meant conversion: the process of *metanoia,* or radical change of life, was involved. Through penance, Christians demonstrated their predisposition to be once more entirely faithful to the commitments they had assumed. This process was called *exomologese* ("penitential discipline"). The precondition for penance was the acknowledgment of the truth: the candidate for reconciliation must be capable of self-criticism, of an integral recognition of his or her lapse.

Cyprian considered it basic that those who had been guilty of misconduct should not be reconciled immediately, but should first do penance. To fail to proceed in this fashion, he felt, was equivalent to undervaluing the disposition of steadfastness and fidelity.

Worse, it entailed the risk of seeing candidates fall anew, in case they were arrested again. Penance was not just a humiliation, nor was it intended simply as a way of burdening someone with great privation. It was a personal training in detachment, in love for one's brothers and sisters, in self-renunciation, in communion with Christ. The penitent must now become capable of facing new difficulties should they arise. It was a matter of realistic conversion—of changing one's life and turning it in the direction of the Lord: "Rend your hearts, not your garments" (Joel 2:13) (Cyprian, De Lapsis, chap. 29, in Actas de los Mártires, p. 590). It was by an austere, radically evangelical life that a person performed penance. Penance meant despoiling oneself of the encumbrance of possessions, escaping wealth, and placing oneself at the service of others, especially the poor. Concern with food, drink, and clothing, and unconcern for the poor, were incompatible with penance. The penitent was someone who had set aside selfish practice for good and all, to make of his or her life a permanent oblation to God and service to one's sisters and brothers instead.

The penitential period could be abbreviated or prolonged. Once it was over, if the penitents' evangelical dispositions recommended it, they could be fully reintegrated into common life with the brothers and sisters. The criterion for reconciliation was self-criticism in practice. The penitential period could last for months or even years, depending on the gravity of one's apostasy. There were degrees of gravity, as we have seen. Some apostates had lapsed only after prolonged torture. Others had done so without even being threatened, out of simple fear. Still others had purchased a certificate, or sent a pagan friend to the altar as a substitute. Only when penitents had demonstrated their readiness to face up to a new persecution were they readmitted to full community with the other Christians. It was the community as a whole that rendered a judgment on their behavior during the time of penance, and accepted them or rejected them after it was over. Only when the community had handed down its verdict was the penitent readmitted, or refused reconciliation. For example, the attitude of the community toward those lapsi who had conducted themselves irreproachably when seized a second time was that they should be readmitted at once to full communion: here, penance—conversion—had already been done.

However, reconciliation could be granted once only. A new lapse meant exclusion from the church, on grounds that such individuals, too attached to their possessions, family, or own person, and "loving their own life more than Christ," gave evidence of ineptitude for the Christian life.

It is important to note the similarity between the penitential period and the catechumenate. Both were a time of probation, a period of testing. Demands were more severe for reconciliation, because the subject had demonstrated something less than a full capacity for the practice of the Christian life, and it was crucial to verify serious conversion. But in both penance and the catechumenate, the community played a key role. In both, the criterion of verification was *practice* and *life*. (See Cyprian, *The Lapsed,* in *Actas de los Mártires,* pp. 560–97; idem, *Letters,* in *Actas de los Mártires,* pp. 472 559; Daniélou and Marrou, *The First Six Hundred Years,* pp. 135, 175; Lebreton and Zeiller, *De la fin du IIe. siècle,* pp. 78–85, 192–96, 341–43.)

The life of the church in the first three centuries of our era is, as we see, an inexhaustible treasury of testimony, fidelity, and creativity. Numerous other examples and testimonials could have been cited here, and they deserve to be better known, but it would have taken us too far afield. What is important for our purposes is to be able to sift out, from among all the things we could learn from the experience of our first sisters and brothers, what will be of most utility for our own Christian living and for the renewal and witness of the church as a whole.

Let me, then, list a few considerations suggested by this study. The church was born amid persecution, was born of Christ's death on the cross at the hands of Jewish and Roman power, and of his resurrection. From the first moments of its existence, it was presented with a mighty challenge: in order to be faithful to Christ, in order to be faithful to the gospel, the church was going to have to take steps to safeguard its freedom amid the harshness of persecution. At no moment could there be any thought of concession, because this could only be at the price of denying Christ, which would be tantamount to the church's own denial of itself. The church would have surrendered the very reason for its existence.

The church had as yet no experience of power. It was still a church of the people, and at the mercy of the whims of the imperial power. From the latter it received no support at all. Further, it was numerically weak at first. Its only bulwark was its loyalty to Christ and the authenticity of its example. The pagans, with their polytheistic beliefs and superstitions, their religion of formality, their decadent morality, and their values centered on material goods and sensuality, felt no attraction for Christianity. Nor did the gospel attract them, with its story of a God who had died and an absurd account of a resurrection from the dead. The gospel broke with idolatrous pagan values, placing the worth of human beings within themselves (freedom, truth, love), broke with social prejudices and divisions (male/female, Jew/Greek, slave/owner), and proposed love and justice as the norm of social life. Further: when the church was subjected to constant persecution, it grew uninterruptedly. Evidently, what led pagans to conversion was solely the witness of the life of Christians and the strength of their faith.

In the first two centuries especially, Christians came from among the poor. Their leaders belonged to these same classes. They did not rise a rung or two on the social ladder when they were chosen for the function of leadership. The tip of the pyramid and the base, then, lived the same basic problematic of life, lived a life of toil and suffering. They all sought solutions to their problems in the means at their disposal, the means of the poor. They could not count on wealth, hence their collections for the very poorest, their sharing of goods, their mutual assistance funds. It was their leaders, furthermore, who were first singled out for repression. And so these had really to be leaders, for it was they who gave the communities their courage, thrust, and dynamism, guiding the church ever to the fore. The pastors were truly the vanguard of the church.

Of course, the persecution reached all. The result was that the Christian criterion of personal value came to be centered on one's practice. Personal worth was not correlated with one's function in the community or one's education. Personal worth was seen in one's manner of life. The demands of the catechumenate, like those of the penitential discipline, show this very well. The community shared in the selection of its leaders, the determination of candidates for baptism, and the reconciliation of the *lapsi,* the "fallen." In other words, Christians were responsible both for their faith and for the church.

The sufferings inflicted on the church by the empire formed Christians of moral fiber. The continual raids by police and soldiers, the destruction of books and homes, the confiscation of property, flight, prison, death, the loss of community leaders—all this obliged the church to live in a state of permanent rootlessness. Nothing was stable, nothing lasting. The church learned to live in insecurity, learned to live provisionally, and learned not to grow attached to property, not to cling to the present. It had really to live by faith in the Lord, the one savior and deliverer, by its certain hope in the future and by its love for Christ and the brothers and sisters—a love that was the wellspring of all its joy and felicity. The church was without ties, was free-floating, so to speak—there was no impediment to its continual renewal in response to whatever needs might arise. It was free to answer the call of history.

The church received no honor or privileges from secular power. It did not depend on that power for its subsistence or its works. On the contrary, the secular authority was an obstacle to its existence, restricting Christians, at the very least, when it did not seize and kill them. The church had to develop "on its own," relying solely on the power of the Spirit. Its independence of secular power gave it total freedom to proclaim the truth, and even to criticize the imperial authority.

The concern of the church was not with its own physical survival. Otherwise it would have had to suspend preaching the gospel. It trusted in the word of the Lord, who had guaranteed that the forces of evil would not prevail against it. It believed that life sprang from death. It hoped against hope: that is, it hoped when no one could have foreseen that, of all things, it would one day be accepted by the whole empire. It believed that through confession and martyrdom it was gaining the victory, and that this was how the power of God was being made manifest.

The life of the primitive church should furnish food for thought. How can we give the church of today the shape and form it will need in order to be faithful to the mission that Christ has confided to it—"You are to be my witnesses in Jerusalem, throughout Judea and Samaria, yes, even to the ends of the earth" (Acts 1:18)?

CHAPTER 4

Hope amid Persecution: A Reading of the Book of Revelation for Today

AUTHORSHIP AND STRUCTURE OF THE BOOK

The author of the Book of Revelation, he tells us himself, is someone named John (Rev. 1:1). He writes from the island of Patmos, in exile, as a scourge rages over the church. The precise identity of this author is still being discussed. Most scholars, in view of the similarities with and differences from the other writings attributed to the Apostle John, hold that the author of Revelation is a member of the circle of the Apostle John, the circle that also produced the fourth Gospel and the three Joannine Letters.

The Book of Revelation is addressed to the "seven churches of Asia Minor"—roughly, what today is called Turkey. Certainly it was that region that produced the text, as we learn from its particular Christian spirit and manner of expression. Doubtless there were more than seven Christian communities in Asia Minor. The number seven is here used symbolically: seven stands for totality, completeness, perfection. The "seven churches" represent the church as a whole.

The author refers to himself as a prophet (Rev. 1:3) under the obligation of sharing with his brothers and sisters the revelation he has received from Jesus Christ. He writes of what he has "seen": of what now is and of what is to occur, the present and the future (1:19). In the events of history, he reads the presence of God. He uncovers a divine meaning in history—he discerns what God thinks and wills.

God's designs come to our prophet-author in the form of visions, which he consigns to writing. It is not these visions, however, that are the *object* of the revelation. The visions *evoke* the revelation, through their symbolism. Hence the great number of visions we encounter in his book, and the myriad of symbols they use. Practically the whole of the Book of Revelation is symbolical. Its numbers, its colors, its personages, its descriptions—all its details conspire to convey a certain revelation. In order to understand the meaning of the text, then, we must translate these symbols into the concepts that the author seeks to transmit.

Most exegetes think that the Book of Revelation was written in two stages. The first redaction was produced in the time of Nero, during the first persecution, which began in A.D. 64. The final redaction seems to belong to the time of Domitian, during the second persecution, around A.D. 95 (see Acts 17:10–11).

From a structural viewpoint, Revelation is neatly divided into two parts. The first, chapters 1–3, consists of the letters to the seven churches. There is only one vision here, that of the "Son of Man," which introduces the letters. The letters are an analysis of the respective situations of the seven communities. They contain praise, counsel, admonition, and a ceaseless appeal for loyalty. By contrast, the second part, chapters 4–22—the "revelation" as such—is simply a series of visions, one following upon the other almost without any moralizing.

The visions of the second part of Revelation bear primarily on the future: "what must happen very soon" (Acts 1:1). Two subdivisions can be clearly distinguished in this second part. In the first subdivision, chapters 4–11, "John" sets forth the signs that are to appear at the end of the ages. Amid wars and catastrophes of all kinds, including cosmic ones, salvation will appear, in the form of the deliverance and liberation of the persecuted Christians. There are certain references to the church, but only in passing, and in anticipation of the second subdivision.

In the second subdivision, chapters 12–22, the persecutions come on the scene, in all their violent drama. Now we read of the fate of the persecuted church, and the writer seeks to respond more directly to the anguish of his fellow Christians. The images become clearer. The present state of the world, along with the future of the persecutors and of the church, unfold symbolically before our eyes. The Book of Revelation ends with visions describing Christ's victory, the last judgment, and the final kingdom of glory.

Revelation, then, was written at a time when the church was suffering persecution. The Roman empire is persecuting Christians because they refuse to worship the emperors. For the Christians there is only one Lord God, Jesus Christ. But "Lord God" happens precisely to be the title now accorded the Roman emperor. Statues of the emperor were being erected, and a whole imperial cultus was spreading apace. The city of Pergamum, for instance, was the center of this cult in Asia Minor. "I know you live in the very place where Satan's throne is erected" (Rev. 2:13). The religion of the empire—a form of paganism now including emperor worship—was the fundamental element of cohesion of all its domains. Through its religion, the empire maintained unity. The presence of a group of persons who refused to submit to its religion was viewed as overt hostility, and persecution was inevitable. Christians were led to the tribunals, to death at the stake, to the circus to be devoured by wild beasts. Saint Peter and Saint Paul were victims of persecution, martyred at the time of Nero.

Of this historical situation the Book of Revelation is born. It is a *message of hope.* The church was living in a time of insecurity. There were prisons and executions. Communities lost their leaders. The suffering and travail were great. Inevitably, there was anguish and confusion. What would the future bring? Would there be a future? The faith was shaken in some Christians. Present shock obscured future hope. If Christ had conquered in his resurrection, if he had overcome the world (John 16:33), then how came such slaughter of his own?

The Book of Revelation seeks to respond to this problematic. It seeks to open horizons, strengthen faith, give solid reasons for hope. It arrives on the scene with an injection of courage. It is a cry for steadfastness, for struggle, for resistance. It is a call to battle. Throughout, it is an encomium of fighters, of martyrs, of those who have given their lives for a witness. We might say that Revelation limns a theology of persecution.

It is a *theology of the church in the world.* The Christian option for a radical attachment to Jesus Christ has immediate consequences in the political sphere. This is altogether clear in the Book of Revelation. Being a Christian is no neutral option. On the contrary, it calls for attitudes that provoke ever stronger reactions. Obstacles arise at every turn. Danger is ever-present. The Christian life is conceived as a struggle, and Christians must be prepared for what they will have to confront. Christians may be sure of one thing, however: Christ's is the final victory.

Finally, Revelation is a *theology of history*. It presents history as a battlefield where two great adversaries meet: the Christians, faithful to Christ and to God, and the oppressors with their followers, the minions of the prince of evil. On the one side we have those in quest of the realization of the kingdom of justice and love. On the other we have those who are doing their best to prevent it. At certain moments the oppressors, giving vent to their evil designs, dominate and crush the Christians. The evil they unleash is the occasion of the witness of martyrdom. But God presides over history, supervises its whole development: "The kingdom of the world now belongs to our Lord and to his Annointed One, and he shall reign forever and ever" (Rev. 11:15). Despite opposing powers, despite all those who throw up obstacles in the way of the kingdom for which Christians strive, God is bringing history to its full realization.

These are the notions that we see developed throughout this final book of the Bible, and these are the notions that I shall attempt to develop in my explanation. The objective of my book is not to explain all of the visions and symbols of the Book of Revelation separately. Innumerable books have done this already. My concern is to show the relevance of the Book of Revelation for today and to carry its message to the world of today. I hope to show that the validity of its message is not limited to the historical era in which it was written, but that it extends to all times, that it is perennial.

THE PERSECUTORS

Then another sign appeared in the sky: it was a huge dragon, flaming red, with seven heads and ten horns; on his heads were seven diadems. . . . Enraged at [the woman's] escape, the dragon went off to make war on the rest of her offspring, on those who keep God's commandments and give witness to

Jesus. . . . Then I saw a wild beast come out of the sea with ten horns and seven heads; on its horns were ten diadems and on its heads blasphemous names. . . . I saw a woman seated on a scarlet beast which was covered with blasphemous names. This beast had seven heads and ten horns. . . . On her forehead was written a symbolic name, "Babylon the great, mother of harlots and all the world's abominations." I saw that the woman was drunk with the blood of God's holy ones and the blood of those martyred for their faith in Jesus. . . . Then I saw another wild beast come up out of the earth; it had two horns like a ram and it spoke like a dragon. [Rev. 12:3, 17; 13:1; 17:3, 5–6; 13:11].

Here, symbolically, are the persecutors of the church. The dragon is evil personified, the power that animates oppressive might. The heads, horns, and diadems symbolize now kings, now emperors, according to the literary context. The horns and diadems are symbols of power. Scarlet is the color of blood, of murder, of the persecuting might. The woman hated by the dragon symbolizes the church. Her offspring are the Christians. The harlot is Rome, prototype of power that persecutes. She is called Babylon because of Roman idolatry and persecution of God's people, just as with Babylon in the Old Testament: it was Babylon that laid seige to Jerusalem and enslaved and deported the Jews. Prostitution is a constant theme with the prophets. It designates the worship of false gods—idolatry. The idol is a substitute for God, something besides God to which divine power is attributed. Rome is the mother of harlots because Rome seeks to draw all human beings to the worship of false values. The first beast, to which the dragon gives its power, is the Roman empire, or, more broadly, oppressive political might. The second beast symbolizes religious power and might, divinizing the first beast and acting as its mouthpiece for purposes of propaganda. Let us examine the characteristics of these symbolic creatures in more detail.

Another passage is more precise about who the Christians' enemies are: "the kings of the earth, the nobles and those in command, the wealthy and powerful, the slave and the free" (Rev. 6:15). The empire included innumerable dominated powers, which were allowed to retain their kings and their wealthy classes, though they were all subject to Rome. These are the "slave" powers. The enemies, then, are those with economic, political, or military power who utilize this power to oppress and exploit, to destroy and dominate. It is they who, when they encounter resistance on the part of Christians, employ force to extirpate them from the face of the earth. "Are not the rich exploiting you? They are the ones who hale you into the courts and who blaspheme that noble name which has made you God's own" (James 2:6–7).

For the rich and powerful, happiness is found in material satisfaction. The meaning of life is in riches, wealth, comfort, and pleasure. The mighty and the wealthy place their trust in material goods and bodily satisfactions. It is in these that they put their trust. "The woman was dressed in purple and scarlet and adorned with gold and pearls and other jewels. In her hand she held a gold cup that was filled with the abominable and sordid deeds of her lewdness" (Rev. 17:4). These are the values in which the wealthy and the mighty believe: money and luxury. The value and worth of an individual is no longer found within that individual, but in what he or she possesses. It is a person's possessions, appearance, social condition, and "culture" that render that person great. The rich and mighty worship "gods made from gold and silver, from bronze and stone and wood, which cannot see or hear or walk" (Rev. 9:20).

There are those who think that these things can make them great and save them! They believe in their capabilities, and are fooled by their deceitful powers. They submit to them, they allow themselves to be dominated and guided by them. They become the slaves of things, and from them expect all their felicity. "Of what remains [of the wood he has burned for cooking and heating] he makes a god, his idol, and prostrate before it in worship, he implores it, 'Rescue me, for you are my god' " (Isa. 44:17).

These are the ones who expect to find deliverance and liberation—fulfillment itself—in their own goods and property. They live in a state of seduction—seduction by external values. In their state of delusion, they fail to perceive that such objects and sensations are incapable of fulfilling their capacity for love. And so they must always have more. They are never satisfied with what they have. They replace one object with another, they are forever augmenting their possessions and trying out new forms of pleasure, for no one of them is enough. These are idols that are "the handiwork of men" (Ps. 135:15), and hence cannot satisfy them. Human beings thirst for might and wealth, and this thirst can be slaked only at others' cost. They can accumulate goods only through exploitation. "It is you who have devoured the vineyard; the loot wrested from the poor is in your house" (Isa. 3:14). "Their houses are as full of treachery as a bird-cage is of birds; therefore they grow powerful and rich, fat and sleek" (Jer. 5:27). They abduct other human beings to do them service. They "work their neighbor without pay, and give him no wages" (Jer. 22:13). They suck others dry, drain their strength. They enslave them. This is possible only in an oppressive political regime. They demean persons, they trim them down, they make them do their will. In order to obtain the complete subjection of other human beings and their perfect integration into their own objectives, they develop an immense propaganda mechanism. They must convince others that they can be fulfilled only through the possession of material goods, that human beings are fully human only in proportion to what they have. They must persuade them to worship idols—to worship the beast that procures this kind of life for them:

> Then I saw another wild beast come up out of the earth; it had two horns like a ram and it spoke like a dragon. ["Be on your guard against false prophets, who come to you in sheep's clothing but underneath are wolves on the prowl"—Matt. 7:15.] It used the authority of the first beast to promote its interests by making the world and all its inhabitants worship the first beast. . . . Because of the prodigies it was allowed to perform by authority of the first beast, it led astray the earth's inhabitants [Rev. 13:11–14].

Deceived and insatiable, men and women enter the race for wealth, the unbridled quest for material things, to fulfill their desire for happiness. And in so doing they transform both themselves and their fellow human beings into objects. They become objects themselves, in that their self-worth is no longer within themselves, but is in what they possess. They make objects of their fellow human beings, in that they use them to obtain what they desire. They transform themselves into things, and things come to be worshiped. It is now things that command relationships among persons. "They . . . went after empty idols and became empty themselves" (Jer. 2:5).

To be effective, dominion must be total. Those who are not seduced must be forced. Those who do not submit of their own free will must be economically coerced. If they still resist, they are to be eliminated:

> The second wild beast was then permitted to give life to the beast's image, so that the image had the power of speech and of putting to death anyone who refused to worship it. It forced all men, small and great, rich and poor, slave and free, to accept a stamped image on their right hand or their forehead. Moreover, it did not allow a man to buy or sell anything unless he was first marked with the name of the beast or with the number that stood for its name [Rev. 13:15-17].

"The image had the power of speech": the idol must be as realistic as possible in order to be able to deceive the unwary.

Oppressors are called "those who lay the earth waste" (Rev. 11:18). There are no limits to the measures they are willing to take to achieve their ends. They repress, they murder. They not only throw human beings in chains, they prevent life itself from growing and developing, making the whole world fodder for their voracious appetites. "And on its heads [were] blasphemous names. . . . The [first] beast was given a mouth for uttering proud boasts and blasphemies" (Rev. 13:1, 5). The powerful pine after the place of God—they arrogate to themselves the titles that are meet for God, and not for human beings. They usurp the right of life and death, they wield repressive power in such a way as to intimidate everyone. No consideration suffices to turn them from their regime of death. Here is the historical realism of the Book of Revelation: oppressors do not easily change their minds. Despite all the signs of the times, "neither did they repent of their murders or their sorcery, their fornication or their thefts" (Rev. 9:21).

All those who share in any way in the advantages of power and wealth, goods acquired by the exploitation of other men and women, render their worship to the beast. They cannot escape its clutches. It has become their way of life. In it they place all their hope. "The beast will be worshiped by all those inhabitants of earth who did not have their names written at the world's beginning in the book of the living, which belongs to the Lamb who was slain. . . . They also worshiped the beast and said, 'Who can compare with the beast, or come forward to fight against it?' " (Rev. 13:8, 4). They are so drunk with power that they see their dominion as eternal.

UNBRIDLED PERSECUTION

Christians rebel against this state of things. They refuse to accept such an abasement of human beings. They will not submit to idolatry and prostitution. They bring everything out into the open, they proclaim the truth, they denounce illusion, they reveal the identity of the true God, of the one who is able to save and deliver. They place the beast in check, all its arrogance notwithstanding. Their resistance, their steadfastness, their witness, the truth they proclaim—all of this bodes trouble for oppressors, all of this threatens to stir the passive from their torpor, all of this bids fair to block oppressors' pretensions. This constitutes a serious threat to the prevailing power structure: it may be dissolved. And so dominators intensify their persecution: "The beast was allowed to wage war against God's people and conquer them" (Rev. 13:7). All those in the beast's retinue, all who share in its profits and its conception of life, hate Christians for this attitude of theirs. And so, when Christians are eliminated by oppression, they "gloat over them and in their merriment exchange gifts, because these . . . prophets harassed everyone on earth" (Rev. 11:10).

The Book of Revelation is preoccupied from beginning to end with one thing: persecution. Its solemn exordium gives fair warning: "I, John, your brother, who share with you the *distress* and the kingly reign and the *endurance* we have in Jesus, found myself on the island called Patmos *because I proclaimed God's word* and bore witness to Jesus" (Rev. 1:9, italics added). The situation of the churches is serious. The common thread running through the author's description is that of their difficulties, their suffering for Christ's sake. In the letter to the church in Ephesus (Rev. 2:1–7), the Lord says, "I know your deeds, your labors, and your patient endurance. . . . You are patient and endure hardship for my cause"

(vv. 2–3). In the letter to the church in Smyrna (Rev. 2:8–11) he says, "I know of your tribulation and your poverty, even though you are rich. I know the slander you endure. . . . Have no fear of the sufferings to come. The devil will indeed cast some of you into prison to put you to the test; you will be tried over a period of ten days" (vv. 9–10); and to the church in Pergamum (Rev. 2:12–17) he says, "I know you live in the very place where Satan's throne is erected; and I know you hold fast to my name and have not denied the faith you have in me, not even at the time when Antipas, my faithful witness, was martyred in your city where Satan has his home" (v. 13). And so on. This, then, is the situation, and these the resultant problems. This is what the revelation of God's judgments will respond to.

Chapter eleven furnishes us with a nutshell history of the church. Let us examine it closely:

> Someone gave me a measuring rod and said: "Come and take the measurements of God's temple and altar, and count those who worship there. Exclude the outer court of the temple, however; do not measure it, for it has been handed over to the Gentiles, who will crush the holy city for forty-two months. I will commission my two witnesses to prophesy for those twelve hundred and sixty days, dressed in sackcloth."
>
> These are the two olive trees and the two lampstands which stand in the presence of the Lord of the earth. If anyone tries to harm them, fire will come out of the mouths of these witnesses to devour their enemies. Anyone attempting to harm them will surely be slain in this way. These witnesses have power to close up the sky so that no rain will fall during the time of their mission. They also have power to turn water into blood and to afflict the earth at will with any kind of plague.
>
> When they have finished giving their testimony, the wild beast that comes up from the abyss will wage war against them and conquer and kill them. Their corpses will lie in the streets of the great city, which has the symbolic name "Sodom" or "Egypt," where also their Lord was crucified. Men from every people and race, language and nation, stare at their corpses for three and a half days but refuse to bury

them. The earth's inhabitants gloat over them and in their merriment exchange gifts, because these two prophets harassed everyone on earth. But after the three and a half days, the breath of life which comes from God returned to them. When they stood on their feet sheer terror gripped those who saw them. The two prophets heard a loud voice from heaven say to them, "Come up here!" So they went up to heaven in a cloud as their enemies looked on. At that moment there was a violent earthquake and a tenth of the city fell in ruins. Seven thousand persons were killed during the earthquake; the rest were so terrified that they worshiped the God of heaven [Rev. 11:1–13].

Here we have the various elements in the history of the church: persecution, its causes, the persecutors, and Christian victory. Let us examine the symbols used in the passage. "God's temple" and "those who worship there" are the church. The measuring of the temple indicates that God will protect it. The "gentiles" and the "earth's inhabitants" are the retinue of those who oppress and persecute the Christians. This is likewise the sense of "world" in various passages of Saint John's gospel: "If you find that the world hates you, know it has hated me before you" (John 15:18). The "outer court of the temple" is the body, the only part of the Christian that repression can affect. The "holy city" is the New Jerusalem, symbol of the church. The "two witnesses" are likewise the church, this time in its mission of testimony to Jesus Christ, its task of being the mouthpiece of God's judgments. The twelve hundred sixty days," or "forty-two months" (three and one-half years), or "three and a half days" symbolize the time of the duration of the persecution. It is also the age of the church, how old the church is up to this time. Hence we learn that as long as the church is active, it will face tribulation. The "prophets" are girded with divine power, the strength of God present in them. The city called "Sodom" or "Egypt" is the seat of oppressive power. Egypt is the prototype of the oppressive nation: it enslaved the Israelites for four hundred years. Sodom represents depravity, dissolute customs, corruption. These are traits of the seat of the empire. "Every people and race, language and nation" is a stereotyped formula to designate universality. It is the same as saying "all peoples." "Three and a half days" is an imperfect time—half of seven, which is perfection—and denotes something temporary, of short duration, not definitive.

Let us attempt to sound the depths of the message of this passage. The outer court "has been handed over to the Gentiles, who will crush the holy city for forty-two months." And the wild beast "will wage war against them and conquer and kill them." There is nothing strange about persecution in the life of the church. It is to be expected. "No pupil outranks his teacher, no slave his master. . . . If they call the head of the house Beelzebul, how much more the members of his household!" (Matt. 10:24–25). "They will harry you as they harried me" (John 15:20). This theme reappears in the Book of Revelation again and again. The consequences of the Christian option are clearly perceived. "Each of the martyrs was given a long white robe, and they were told to be patient a little while longer until the quota was filled of their fellow servants and brothers to be slain, as they had been" (Rev. 6:11).

The outlook of the church must always include the prospect of persecution. And yet so many are scandalized when this occurs! They think that something has gone wrong, that the church and the powers that be should always bask in peaceful coexistence. Disagreement, imprisonment, torture, exile, flight, death, censorship, imposed silence—all this comes as a sudden shock, as if the mystery of the cross were not the center of the Christian message, as if Christ's sufferings were his alone, or as if Jesus' trial and sentencing were somehow necessary for redemption but without having any connection with subsequent historical reality, with political powers, with dominant classes.

The Book of Revelation is realistic: an option for Christ leads to an attitude of life with immediate consequences on the level of social and political life. Witness to Christ is not neutral. It is a sign of contradiction (Luke 2:34). It means taking a stand. "Do you think I have come to establish peace on the earth? I assure you, the contrary is true; I have come for division" (Luke 12:51). Whenever someone bears witness to Christ, others make up their minds. They decide. They take one side or the other. There is no possibility of indifference. "Indifference" itself is an attitude: "He who is not with me is against me, and he who does not gather with me scatters" (Luke 11:23).

The reason for disturbance is clear: "these two prophets harassed everyone on earth." The function of a prophet—the function of the church in its prophetical capacity—is to proclaim God's designs for reality, for events. It is to declare the truth. Prophets tear off masks, rip through the fantasies with which so many persons cloak reality, reveal the truth that lies beneath appearances. They refuse to leave the complacent at peace—at peace with their consciences. They stir their complacency, and their selfish oppression of others, to the dregs. How annoying! And so the unjust are not left in "peace" to accomplish their designs, no longer have "freedom" to practice their injustices. All now know that their works are not authentic, that their only purpose is their perpetrators' own advantage, to the detriment of others. Christians disturb such a nicely constructed empire. An "order" built on injustice, a Pax Romana based on authoritarianism and coercion, feels its foundations shake.

The authors of oppression, those who share the privileges of might and wealth, cannot tolerate such an offense. They will brook no obstacle to their intent. It is not that Christians simply bear some stigma, are somehow mysteriously marked for persecution. Their persecution is for altogether concrete reasons. A despotic power feels threatened, and will feel secure only when the disturbers have been eliminated, and so it unleashes its oppression. In order to maintain themselves in power, oppressors crush their opposers. Christians, then, need not wonder at the trials they face. These are so foreseeable, so certain, that they become one of the gospel beatitudes: "Blest are you when they insult you and persecute you and utter every kind of slander against you because of me. Be glad and rejoice, for your reward is great in heaven; they persecuted the prophets before you in the very same way" (Matt. 5:11-12).

"I saw that the woman [the great harlot] was drunk with the blood of God's holy ones and the blood of those martyred for their faith in Jesus" (Rev. 17:6). All who will not submit, who resist and remain steadfast, are fated to suffer and even die by the oppressor's hand. "Anyone who wants to live a godly life in Christ Jesus can expect to be persecuted" (2 Tim. 3:12). Those who refuse to be enticed by the illusions of dominators, or who are unwilling to humble themselves obediently before their absolute dominion, must be broken, eliminated. The Christian way of life, its prophetic witness, calls into question all totalitarianism, all lordship that arrogates unto itself the power of life and death. It challenges—denies—the divine quality of such lordship—its right (acquired by force) to subjugate. Christians denounce all of this as farcical. And from that moment their life is at stake. Their peril is their very milieu. Their very existence is theirs no longer. "He died for all so that those who live might live no longer for themselves, but for him who for their sakes died and was raised up" (2 Cor. 5:15). The raison d'être of their lives is the good of others. Their prime concern is the common good. If human values are at stake, then, if persons are subjected to subhuman treatment, Christians are ready to run risks to defend them.

The First Letter of Peter furnishes us with a fine synthesis of the Christian position in the face of persecution:

Do not be surprised, beloved, that a trial by fire is occurring in your midst. It is a test for you, but it should not catch you off guard. Rejoice instead, in the measure that you share Christ's sufferings. When his glory is revealed, you will rejoice exultantly. Happy are you when you are insulted for the sake of Christ, for then God's Spirit in its glory has come to rest on you. See to it that none of you suffers for being a murderer, a thief, a malefactor, or a destroyer of another's rights. If anyone suffers for being a Christian, however, he ought not to be ashamed. He should rather glorify God in virtue of that name [1 Pet. 4:12–16].

THE CHALLENGE OF PERSECUTION

I know . . . your patient endurance. . . . Have no fear of the sufferings to come. . . . I know you hold fast to my name and have not denied the faith you have in me. . . . Because you have kept my plea to stand fast, I will keep you safe in the time of trial which is coming on the whole world, to test all men on earth. I am coming soon. Hold fast to what you have [your faith]" [Rev. 2:2, 10, 13; 3:10–11].

Persecution is a purifying fire, a moment of great tribulation, the great test. The martyrs are "the ones who have survived the great period of trial" (Rev. 7:14). Persecution is the supreme test of faith, the true temptation against fidelity. It is a time of suffering, of the absence of peace, and of only short-term tranquility. There is no hope of security in the near future. Everything is crashing about one's ears, the earth dissolves underfoot, faith is rocked to its foundations. Hence the reiterated appeal for steadfastnesses, hence the urgings to be consistent with one's faith, without hesitancy, and to bear witness to the very end. But the appeal goes hand in hand with eschatological promises: "Hold fast to what you have until I come. To the one who wins the victory, who keeps to my ways till the end, I will give authority over the nations—the same authority I received from my Father" (Rev. 2:25–26). They are the same appeals that Christ addresses to his followers in the gospel: "You will be hated by all on account of me. But whoever holds out till the end will escape death" (Matt. 10:22).

This is the trial that strains faith to the limit, testing to what pitch each person has really placed his or her life at God's disposition, spurning death itself, to what point one's option for love, for the building of a new world, one's self-abandon into the Lord's hands, is deeply, solidly rooted—or is like the seed that fell on rocky soil (Matt. 13:20). In moments of calm, all this can pass unnoticed. Now it must come into the open. The time has arrived to "say 'Yes' when you mean 'Yes' and 'No' when you mean 'No' " (Matt. 5:37). And so each of the seven letters in chapters 2 and 3 of Revelation ends with a promise to the "victor." This is all a battle, then! The victor in the battle is the one who holds out to the end:

> I will make the victor a pillar in the temple of my God and he shall never leave it. I will inscribe on him the name of my God and the name of the city of my God, the new Jerusalem which he will send down from heaven, and my own name which is new. Let him who has ears heed the spirit's word to the churches! [Rev. 3:12–13].

In the Bible, a name is not a simple conventional designation, a mere title. A name expresses the role a person performs, the activity or the destiny of the person who bears that name. A name is not something neutral. It expresses *what a person is.* To act upon someone's name implies power over that person. To change someone's name is to give him or her a new personhood, a new destiny, a definitive connection with some other person. God changes a person's name to indicate that God is taking possession of the life of this Christian: that person's future is now definitively linked to God, linked to a share in divine happiness. A new name signifies conversion and surrender to Christ.

Patience, in the sense of steadfastness or constancy, is the great virtue of the persecuted. It expresses the attitude of the Christian who hopes and perseveres. Through patience Christians await the coming of Christ, who will lead them to the kingdom and join them to God. This expectation and sure hope of Christ's coming is translated in practice into perseverance and fidelity in the face of present difficulties and hardships. The root of patience, then, is faith in the Jesus who comes, and its salient trait is the inner strength that makes it possible for someone to persevere. In practice, patience is steadfastness in the face of persecution. This is why Paul could write: "We even boast of our afflictions! We know that affliction makes for endurance, and endurance for tested virtue, and tested virtue for hope" (Rom. 5:3–4).

Precisely as an age of catastrophe and harsh confrontation, a time of persecution becomes a time of serious danger—the danger of discouragement: "You are patient and endure hardship for my cause. Moreover, you do not become discouraged" (Rev. 2:3). Defeat does not consist in being tortured or killed, but in giving up, wearing out, yielding points, going over to the other side. The temptation to yield is great, and intensifies in proportion to the degree of the tribulation to be endured. One must be prepared, one must be secure in one's union with Christ, and detached from all possessions, life included. One may not vacillate or compromise. Compromise is actually switching sides, by making concessions to the other side: "I know your deeds; I know you are neither hot nor cold! But because you are lukewarm, neither hot nor cold, I will spew you out of my mouth!" (Rev. 3:15–16).

Hesitation means that the option for Christ has not been total. You must surrender yourself entirely, for the test will be a difficult one. Many fail to bear up under the heavy weight of the trial and begin to play a double game. They no longer draw out the gospel to the whole radicality of its consequences. And so they cease to proclaim the truth aloud. They omit parts of it. They assume attitudes of false prudence. They make the concessions necessary for survival.

Attachment to life, or even to the survival of an institution, now takes precedence over witness. Attachment to privileges, to comfort and a "nice life," to positions attained, to property, now prevents Christians from assuming attitudes in conformity with gospel demands, to commitment to the brothers and sisters. The words, "The good shepherd lays down his life for the sheep" (John 10:11), and "There is no greater love than this: to lay down one's life for one's friends" (John 15:13), no longer ring in their ears. They rationalize their cowardice: they find excuses in the gospel itself. They hide beneath formulas, principles, and juridical norms. Their attachment keeps them from the pilgrimage, trammels them, makes them indolent and fickle: "You keep saying, 'I am so rich and secure that I want for nothing.' Little do you realize how wretched you are, how pitiable and poor, how blind and naked!" (Rev. 3:17–letter to the church of Laodicea).

Material riches become an obstacle to total surrender. The rich are incapable of following the inspiration of the Spirit. Situations demand an ever more radical position-taking, and the rich are left behind. They imprison the gospel, they muzzle God's word. Their counterwitness scandalizes others, preventing them from advancing. The fears of the rich paralyze them, and their example obscures the Lord's face. They are no longer instruments of grace. They obstruct the flow of grace.

Persecution, then, is a two-edged sword. It perfects Christians in their option, strengthens them in their witness, enables them to deepen their life with God. At the same time, others are vanquished. They fail the test. They retreat. But on the whole, persecution is like a refiner's fire: the church becomes more authentic, those who have made a true oblation of their lives persevere. And union with God is reinforced. Ostracized, pressured, subjected to countless tribulations, Christians no longer find physical security or support in any material element. They are driven to place their whole trust in the Lord, the one immovable rock: "I love you, O Lord, my strength, O Lord, my rock, my fortress, my deliverer" (Ps. 18:2–3).

In extremity, in the loss of secondary support, one is driven to a clear perception of what is essential, and inspired to concentrate on it. One can no longer run away. There is no longer any compensation, not even a small one. Everything incidental is revealed in all its fragility, its uselessness, its insufficiency. Neither prestige, nor culture, nor property, nor money can save any longer. By contrast, God appears in all might: "I, the Lord, am your God who led you forth from the land of Egypt" (Ps. 81:11). "It is better to take refuge in the Lord than to trust in princes" (Ps. 117:9).

"These are men who have never been defiled by immorality with women. They are pure and follow the Lamb wherever he goes. They have been ransomed as the first fruits of mankind for God and the Lamb" (Rev. 14:4). Prostitution, as we have seen, stands for idolatry. The Israelites, under pressure from other peoples or in difficult situations, sometimes abandoned the worship of the true God and prostrated themselves before idols instead. They took the easy way, they sought other support, other things to rely on. The support they had in God no longer satisfied them. It was too demanding. It called for integrity, consistency, and steadfastness in trial.

The idol that is worshiped today might be survival, in whose name all is sacrificed, even truth itself. Or it might be an important position, finally attained, which one is unwilling to give up, so that now, in its name, one refuses to help brothers and sisters in difficulty. This is an idolatry that results in omission, an omission that leaves the way open to oppressors. Instead of keeping one's gaze, one's confidence, fixed entirely on the Lord—"He only is my rock and my salvation" (Ps. 62:3)—and following the paths that lead to the Lord, one seeks support in seemingly more concrete things, more "dependable" things. Faced with a choice between a "never-failing treasure" (Luke 12:33) and a perishable, but visible and palpable, treasure, it is the latter that is preferred. And from this moment on—that is, from the moment one opts for a secure position, a safe place, the moment there is fear of risk—it is possible and even probable that one will refuse to take correct positions. It is possible to retreat, to strike pacts that should not be struck, and so on. The Nicolaitans (Rev. 2:6) were the heretics who considered it permissible to offer sacrifice to pagan idols in order to escape martyrdom. They considered that the true profession of faith was only in the heart, and not on the lips as well. This was a most serious and lamentable compromise and concession to the forces of oppression.

MISSION OF THE CHURCH: WITNESS

Those who remain faithful and constant run the continual risk of prison and death. But the shedding of their blood joins them in a special way to the Lord and his redemptive sacrifice. Their death purges and purifies them, and makes them particularly worthy of God. Their witness—their *martyrion*—renders Christ's face visible to human beings who have not otherwise known him. "These are the ones who have survived the great period of trial; they have washed their robes and made them white in the blood of the Lamb. It was this that brought them before God's throne; day and night they minister to him in his temple" (Rev. 7:14–15). They are free: in them the word of God encounters no obstacle, and is able to carry out its designs. Their life is an ongoing service of love, which is why they continue to serve after death. It is their love that has led them to this supreme abandonment. They are "virgins" (Rev. 14:4), for they have not defiled themselves with the great harlot or succumbed to the enticements of idols. It was their deprivation that made it possible for them not to become tied down in secondary involvements. Only renunciation gives Christians liberty. Only deprived of all are they capable of moving with the breath of the Spirit, only thus are their feet without shares and chains, as for example in Smyrna: "I know of your tribulation and your poverty, even though you are rich" (Rev. 2:9). Material poverty affords the conditions necessary for empathizing with the sufferings of others, permits mobility, opens the way to service without stint. With nothing to lock up, nothing to fasten down, no possessions to protect, Smyrna is the domain of the freedom of the daughters and sons of God.

This freedom consists in the option for Christ, and for others, to the end. One cannot simply do as one likes; but one can opt for total service, and refuse to retreat in the face of obstacles. This freedom is independent of place, social position, or any other condition. It is to be found even behind prison bars: "In preaching [the gospel] I suffer as a criminal, even to the point of being thrown into chains—but there is no chaining the word of God!" (2 Tim. 2:9). In fact, it is precisely Christian freedom that leads so many to prison and even death, because Christians cannot be intimidated or have their thought or action curtailed by forces opposed to love, forces opposed to human beings, forces that live on the destruction of others. Christians do not purchase their physical liberty, or even their life, at the price of abandoning their faith. This is the freedom we find in Peter and John before the Sanhedrin, when threatened with condemnation: "Surely we cannot help speaking of what we have heard and seen" (Acts 4:20). "Better for us to obey God than men!" (Acts 5:29).

What counts is faith. This is essential, coupled with love for God and service to one's sisters and brothers. This is worth the sacrifice of all the rest. This is the one permissible attachment: to truth and justice. "Seek out instead his kingship over you, and the rest will follow in turn" (Luke 12:31). For these values, Christians will fight, even though the cross looms as a certainty for those who have chosen this way without reservations. No threat, no repression can make them yield. They are ready to "go the whole way." "On their lips no deceit has been found; they are indeed without flaw" (Rev. 14:5). They have struck no pact, they have accepted no compromise, so as to have their lives spared. They deny neither the Lord nor their brothers and sisters. The freedom of the daughters and sons of God (Rom. 8:21) is the freedom to risk one's external liberty for one's options. This is why "there is no chaining the word of God." The cross is the supreme witness of this freedom that does not measure the sacrifice of service.

Here is a trial, a test, that places the Christian squarely before two options: submit and survive, or refuse to submit, maintain your freedom, and live a life full of risk and insecurity. To take the first option is mediocrity, enslavement to the whims of an inhuman and dehumanizing conception of life. To take the second option means following Christ in his tribulations, holding fast to his mission, resisting the forces of destruction, sharing in the building of a new humankind, and of a new world, in which all human beings will actually be free.

The Book of Revelation seeks precisely to demonstrate that this is the way of the church, and this is why it so lauds the martyrs: "When the Lamb broke open the fifth seal, I saw under the altar the spirits of those who had been martyred because of the witness they bore to the word of God" (Rev. 6:9). This is a eulogy of those who have conducted themselves as Christians, who have followed with steadfastness in the footsteps of the Lamb. They have accepted the consequences of their attachment to Christ, they have taken up his way of winning—which is not through power and domination, but through service and faithfulness to the death. They have suffered, but they have won the victory: "each of the martyrs was given a long white robe" (Rev. 6:11). This is the church's way because it is the Master's way. After all, he is the true light, who has come into the world to enlighten all men and women, and Christians are the followers of that light. And of course the doers of deeds of darkness hate the light: "Men loved darkness rather than light because their deeds were wicked. Eveyone who practices evil hates the light; he does not come near it for fear his deeds will be exposed" (John 3:19–20).

It is by reason of fidelity that the church gains the victory, in the footsteps of Christ: "After this I saw before me a huge crowd which no one could count from every nation and race, people and tongue. They stood before the throne and the Lamb, dressed in long white robes and holding palm branches in their hands" (Rev. 7:9). White is a symbol of purity, gladness, and victory. The palm branches symbolize triumph.

THE RADICAL CHRISTIAN OPTION: CHRIST

For the Christian, Christ is the highest value. From the moment of conversion to Christ, he becomes the Christian's sole possession. "If you seek perfection, go, sell your possessions, and give to the poor. You will then have treasure in heaven. Afterward, come back and follow me" (Matt. 19:21). All else—personal fulfillment, professional satisfaction, comfort, tranquility—becomes secondary. A new pole of attraction begins to function in a Christian's life, giving meaning to all of his or her activities:

> Stop worrying, then, over questions like, "What are we to eat, or what are we to drink, or what are we to wear?" The unbelievers are always running after these things. Your heavenly Father knows all that you need. Seek first his kingship

over you, his way of holiness, and all these things will be given you besides [Matt. 6:31-33].

Most likely, then, tranquility will be lacking, problems will arise, comfort will be at an end, and even persecutions will come. After all, Christians take on the problems of others, fight for truth, devote themselves to the cause of justice. Their personal fulfillment is no longer their individualistic satisfaction. It has become service to their brothers and sisters. And this, with its harshest consequences, is what makes the Christian feel happy and fulfilled. This is what happened in the case of the church of Smyrna—materially poor, despoiled, but rich when it came to the things that count, for the church of Smyrna was rich in love (Rev. 2:9).

"Then, between the throne with the four living creatures and the elders, I saw a Lamb standing, a Lamb that had been slain" (Rev. 5:6). Christ is the Paschal Lamb, immolated for the salvation of the people: God became a human being, and by his death gave life to the world. The Book of Revelation combines the image of the Servant of Yahweh (Isa. 52:13-53:12), who bears the sins of human beings and offers himself as a sacrificial lamb, and the rite of the Passover lamb (Exodus 12), symbol of Israel's redemption. By his death and resurrection, Christ actualizes human freedom, erecting a new people of God, just as the immolation of the lamb in the Old Testament symbolized Israel's deliverance from oppression in Egypt. Now we have a new exodus, victory over the powers of evil, freedom from the forces of oppression (of whom the pharaoh was the prototype). It is Christians, then, who can sing the song of Moses and the Lamb (Rev. 15:3-4), in celebration of their liberation. The Lamb still bears the marks of his torment, indicating the death he died—but he is on his feet, in token of the resurrection. No longer does he appear weak and oppressed. Now he is glorious and powerful. He has vanquished the dominator, and thereby liberated the people. He has shown the road to victory. King of kings, Lord of lords, he rules the world, and is the mainstay of Christians: "Know that I am with you always, until the end of the world!" (Matt. 28:20).

This is the new hymn the "four living creatures and the twenty-four elders" [the church, the heavenly court] sang:

Worthy are you to receive the scroll
and break open its seals,
for you were slain.
With your blood you purchased for God
men of every race and tongue,
of every people and nation.
You made of them a kingdom,
and priests to serve our God,
and they shall reign on the earth [Rev. 5:9–10].

The sealed scroll is the book of the divine decrees regarding the world and its future. Christ receives a special dignity because he gives his life for all humankind. The shedding of his blood confers upon him a higher honor, for this is the greatest proof of love that a human being can offer. This death, this blood, are not in vain. They are liberating. This death, this blood, have led humankind from death to life, from sleep to the dawn, from discouragement to exhilaration and ardor.

There is no love without suffering, no deliverance without sacrifice, no life without death: "Unless the grain of wheat falls to the earth and dies, it remains just a grain of wheat. But if it dies, it produces much fruit" (John 12:24). This is the central message of Christianity. Christ was raised because he gave his life:

Though he was in the form of God,
he did not deem equality with God
something to be grasped at.
Rather, he emptied himself
and took the form of a slave,
being born in the likeness of men.
He was known to be of human estate,
and it was thus that he humbled himself,
obediently accepting even death,
death on a cross!
Because of this,
God highly exalted him
and bestowed on him the name
above every other name.

So that at Jesus' name
  every knee must bend
  in the heavens, on the earth,
  and under the earth,
  and every tongue proclaim
  to the glory of God the Father:
Jesus Christ is Lord! [Phil. 2:6–11].

Christians follow the Lamb for good and all, inebriated with his charisms: "Then the Lamb appeared in my vision. He was standing on Mount Zion, and with him were the hundred and forty-four thousand who had his name and the name of his Father written on their foreheads" (Rev. 14:1). The name on their foreheads signifies membership in the number of those who have made the option for a detached life. Those so signed are the ones who, like Ezekiel (Ezek 9:4) are indignant, and rebel against the abominations they see committed. They cannot remain impassive when they see such injustice. They make a break with oppression, enslavement, and subjection. They reject it utterly. Deprived of all support in things secondary, they join the project of the construction of a new world, in which slavery will no longer be possible, the fashioning of a new humankind capable of unbounded love, the structuring of a new life, without barriers, without prejudice, without discrimination. They know that this is the path to the same opposition as Christ encountered. But "they defeated [the accuser] by the blood of the Lamb and by the word of their testimony; love for life did not deter them from death" (Rev. 12:11). The "accuser" is the dragon. Christ and his followers win victory by self-oblation. It is Christ's self-offering, his love—to the zenith of sacrifice—that motivates the life of Christians. This is what enables them to win, to conquer.

The road to liberation is paved with the deaths of those who have refused to yield before the assaults of the enemy—who have resisted, and who have remained faithful to the deepest yearnings of a humanity being led to its plenitude. This is why death incurred by those giving their lives for the truth does not defeat them. Their death is a font of life—for themselves and for all humankind as well. Every martyrdom causes countless Christians to spring up, just as Christ's death gave birth to the church.

THE CHRISTIAN LIFE AS COMBAT

Christian doggedness, the loyalty of Christians to commitments made to the poor and to the liberation of all men and women, Christian attachment to the truth, provoke the fury of the mighty, of the oppressor: "Enraged at [the woman's] escape, the dragon went off to make war on the rest of her offspring, on those who keep God's commandments and give witness to Jesus" (Rev. 12:17). The book of Revelation portrays a battle unfolding on the field of history—between those who seek to lead history to its full meaning, and those who oppose this in order to satisfy their selfish desires. The Christian life, most clearly, is an ongoing struggle, a struggle to love in a world in which hatred leaves no room to love, a struggle to proclaim the truth in a world in which lying masquerades as truth in order to force itself on men and women, a struggle to resist those who, their purposes thwarted, seek to eliminate witnesses of the light.

Christians, then, must be prepared. The moment of their option for Christ is the moment of their option for the cross. Liberation has a price: "If a man wishes to come after me, he must deny his very self, take up his cross, and begin to follow in my footsteps" (Matt. 16:24). Now we see why both the gospels and the letters of Saint Paul insist so much on courage, steadfastness, perseverance, faithfulness, passing the test, fearlessness. Beginning with the fourth century, much of this sense of confrontation characterizing Christianity will be lost. The institutionalization of Christian life, a life now seen as a set of legal and moral prescriptions and liturgical feasts, will remove the cross from the area of history and relegate it to the merely spiritual plane. By contrast, the Book of Revelation regards the cross entirely from the viewpoint of the Christian life as a struggle in history. The spiritual has an impact on the historical: the mystery of the word made flesh.

This awareness of the forces unleashed against Christian witness is vividly present in Saint Paul, who exhorts his hearers:

Conduct yourselves, then, in a way worthy of the gospel of Christ. If you do, whether I come and see you myself or hear about your behavior from a distance, it will be clear that you are standing firm in unity of spirit and exerting yourselves with one accord for the faith of the gospel. Do not be intimidated by your opponents in any situation [Phil. 1:27–28].

The victors are not the mighty of this world, the heads of oppressor armies, the possessors of lethal weapons. They are the lowly, the weak, the poor, those without visible resources, those who remain steadfast in the perseverance of the faith:

He said to me, "My grace is enough for you, for in weakness power reaches perfection." And so I willingly boast of my weakness instead, that the power of Christ may rest upon me. Therefore I am content with weakness, with mistreatment, with distress, with persecutions and difficulties for the sake of Christ; for when I am powerless, it is then that I am strong [2 Cor. 12:9–10].

When martyrs are delivered up to death, it is Christ who is made manifest in them. And what looks like defeat is exactly the opposite: brute force is incapable of subduing those who have made this radical option. Oppression cannot crush freedom. The one who vanquishes death is the ultimate ruler of the world. Over such a one, the powers of evil can no longer prevail.

HOPE: SEED AND CERTAINTY OF VICTORY

Persecution waxes. The climate is one of anxiety and concern. Uncertainty hangs in the air. And yet in the midst of the tribulation there is hope, a hope stronger than any suffering, a certainty strengthening and animating Christians: "There is nothing to fear. I am the First and the Last and the One who lives. Once I was dead but now I live—forever and ever. I hold the keys of death and the nether world" (Rev. 1:17–18). Here we have the essence of the message of love in the Book of Revelation: Christ lives! Christ has conquered death, and death no longer has dominion over him. This is the certainty that accompanies Christians in all their tribulations: if Christ has vanquished death, he has vanquished it not only for himself, but for all humankind. If Christ has been raised, we shall all be raised with him.

Death is no longer an end, a term. It has been overcome. Now it is fully integrated into the economy of salvation. It is not a "period," as at the end of a sentence, it is a passageway. And death for love, whose model is found in the death of Christ on the cross, entails the certainty of eternal happiness, in the company of the saints in everlasting light. This statement, made by Christians who found themselves surrounded by persecution, subject at every moment to suffering and death, is absolutely basic: if Christ has been raised, then faith is not vain, and the struggle is worth the effort.

Death has been conquered. The forces of evil have no more power over us. Christians can be killed, but only physically. Today is Easter! "He who seeks only himself brings himself to ruin, whereas he who brings himself to nought for me discovers who he is" (Matt. 10:39). Easter, Christ's Passover, signifies precisely that death for love becomes transformed into life: "But after the three and a half days, the breath of life which comes from God returned to them. When they stood on their feet sheer terror gripped those who saw them" (Rev. 11:11). What seems to be the end becomes the seed of new life, the germ of a new world.

The Christian does not look on persecution as a defeat. On the contrary, it is the crowning of his or her struggle, devotion, and toil. It is the natural outcome of a life placed entirely at the service of freedom. Since Christ, no suffering is defeat. It is the outcome of the option of those who have decided to place themselves at the service of the liberation of humanity from all the slaveries to which it is subject.

The central statement of the Book of Revelation is that God is Lord of history:

> A throne was standing there in heaven, and on the throne was seated One whose appearance had a gemlike sparkle as of jasper and carnelian. Around the throne was a rainbow as brilliant as emerald. . . . The twenty-four elders fall down before the One seated on the throne, and worship him who lives forever and ever. They throw down their crowns before the throne and sing:

> O Lord our God, you are worthy
> to receive glory and honor and power!
> For you have created all things;
> by your will they came to be and were made
> [Rev. 4:2–3, 11].

The majestic figure of God seated on the throne permeates the entire book. Ever and again the vision returns: God hovers over the battle waged by the forces of evil against the faithful. God's glorious presence presages victory. No matter what happens, God presides over it:

> Here I stand, knocking at the door. If anyone hears me calling and opens the door, I will enter his house and have supper with him, and he with me. I will give the victor the right to sit with me on my throne, as I myself won the victory and took my seat beside my Father on his throne [Rev. 3:20–21].

Christ is now Lord of history. By virtue of his resurrection, he reigns eternally. Just as no hair of our head falls without God's knowing it, so neither does anything else, any occurrence or deed, escape God's knowledge. To each and all of them God is present, and, though the vagaries of history are numberless, God guides that history toward its objective. In the midst of all difficulties and sufferings, Christ guides the development of history toward the expansion of God's kingdom. In other words, despite all the roadblocks thrown up to interfere with the course of history, history will come to its fullness. Offensives mounted by enemies are useless: they can kill only the body (Luke 12:4). It is the Lord's dominion over history that gives Christians the strength of hope. They are not crestfallen. For they know that, come what may, they will emerge the victors.

ESCHATOLOGICAL VICTORY AND A NEW WORLD

> Then [the mighty of the earth] will come to agreement and bestow their power and authority on the beast. They will fight against the Lamb but the Lamb will conquer them, for he is the Lord of lords and the King of kings; victorious, too, will

be his followers—the ones who were called; the chosen and the faithful [Rev. 17:13-14].

Christians have this guarantee. They have put their trust not in an illusion, not in a chimera, but in the God of might and power able to keep promises to the very end, "the Creator of heaven and earth, the Creator of the sea and the springs" (Rev. 14:7). The Book of Revelation so often contrasts idols, incapable of acting— pure illusions, creations of human beings themselves—with God, who created the world and who acts in history:

> Those who had won the victory over the beast and its image . . . sang . . . : "Mighty and wonderful are your works, Lord God Almighty! . . . Your mighty deeds are clearly seen" [Rev. 15:2-4].

"For he is the living God, enduring forever. . . . He is a deliverer and savior, working signs and wonders in heaven and on earth" (Dan. 6:27-28). No oppression is once and for all, then. No domination is everlasting. The disobedience of oppressors will not abide forever; it is provisional, and destined to lie in ruins. Christians need not despair: times are hard, but in struggle and resistance they will gain the victory. "You will suffer in the world. But take courage! I have overcome the world" (John 16:33).

Even now, in the midst of their apparent victories, oppressors are going down in defeat. It is the witness of love, of the life that conquers death, that is moving history toward its objective. Those who seek to impede it, to throw up obstacles in its path, will enjoy periods of success—and often they will force humanity into a detour, force it into their service, plunging it into selfish concerns and limiting its potential. But the might of the Lord, the might of the resurrection, will ever be present and acting, gradually creating conditions for final victory. The struggle and pain of the present, then, are not without utility. Their purpose will appear. Then shall prevail the kingdom of justice and peace:

> It was this that brought them before God's throne;
>   day and night they minister to him in his temple;
>   he who sits on the throne will give them shelter.

Never again shall they know hunger or thirst,
nor shall the sun or its heat beat down on them,
for the Lamb on the throne will shepherd them.
He will lead them to springs of life-giving water,
and God will wipe every tear from their eyes
[Rev. 7:15–17].

"Then I heard a loud voice in heaven say: 'Now have salvation and power come, the reign of our God and the authority of his Anointed One. For the accuser of our brothers is cast out, who night and day accused them before our God" (Rev. 12:10). Once and for all, evil is routed. It is still present on earth, yes. Christians will yet face persecution and misfortune, yes. But they already possess the power of victory, the might of Christ who walks with them—the certainty that love will triumph:

If God is for us, who can be against us? . . . Who will separate us from the love of Christ? Trial, or distress, or persecution, or hunger, or nakedness, or danger, or the sword? As Scripture says: "For your sake we are being slain all the day long; we are looked upon as sheep to be slaughtered." Yet in all this we are more than conquerors because of him who has loved us. For I am certain that neither death nor life, neither angels nor principalities, neither the present nor the future, nor powers, neither height nor depth nor any other creature, will be able to separate us from the love of God that comes to us in Christ Jesus, our Lord [Rom. 8:31–39].

The Victory

Chapters 19 and 20 of Revelation describe the final combat, the definitive battle—with God, Christ, and their witnesses on one side, and on the other the dragon, the wild beast, and their followers: between truth and the lie, loyalty and corruption.

Rout of the Great Harlot

Alleluia!
Salvation, glory and might belong to our God,
for his judgments are true and just!

He has condemned the great harlot
who corrupted the earth with her harlotry.
He has avenged the blood of his servants
which was shed by her hand [Rev. 19:1–2].

Rout of the Two Beasts

The heavens are opened, and as I looked on, a white horse
appeared; its rider was called "The Faithful and True." Justice is his standard in passing judgment and in waging war.
. . . And his name was the Word of God. . . . Then I saw the
beast and the kings of the earth, and the armies they had
mustered to do battle with the one riding the horse [Christ],
and with his army [the saints]. The beast was captured along
with the false prophet who performed in its presence the
prodigies that led men astray, making them accept the mark
of the beast and worship its image. Both were hurled down
alive into the fiery pool of burning sulphur. The rest were
slain by the sword which came out of the mouth of the One
who rode the horse [Rev. 19:11–21].

Oppressive political power, along with its propaganda arm, that
fomenter of illusion, shall be laid waste. The conqueror rides a
white horse, whose significance we have seen: victory. He is faithful, faithful to death, even death on a cross, and shall be with us
even to the consummation of the ages. He is truth, which brings life
and freedom. He is the word of God, become man and dwelling
among us. The sword that issues from his mouth represents the
devastating decrees of God against the enemies of justice.

Rout of the Dragon

When the thousand years are over, Satan will be released
from his prison. He will go out to seduce the nations in all
four corners of the earth . . . and muster for war the troops
. . . numerous as the sands of the sea. They invaded the
whole country and surrounded the beloved city where God's
people were encamped; but fire came down from heaven and
devoured them. The devil who led them astray was hurled

into the pool of burning sulphur, where the beast and the false prophet had also been thrown. There they will be tortured day and night, forever and ever [Rev. 20:7-10].

The encampment of the saints, the beloved city, symbolizes the church, victim of persecutions. And yet that church will win the victory, through the might of Christ.

The Last Judgment

Judgment has been carried out:

As for the cowards and traitors to the faith, the depraved and murderers, the fornicators and sorcerers, the idol-worshipers and deceivers of every sort—their lot is the fiery pool of burning sulphur, the second death! [Rev. 21:8].

The condemned are those Christians who, from the very outset, retreated from their commitments—who struck an accord with the forces of evil. Faced with repression, the moment they saw the sufferings to which their option was leading them, they yielded to the injunctions of oppressive power, made peace with dominators, and thus obscured the face of Christ the faithful and true. The condemned are especially those who have forced humanity to detour from its true fulfillment, those who elevated slavery to a norm, those who robbed and murdered in order to grow wealthy and powerful, those who lowered human beings to the worship of material goods or physical pleasure as the supreme ideal and guiding norm of their lives.

The first death is physical death, which all must undergo. The second death is death eternal, from which Jesus' witnesses are exempt:

Then I saw some thrones. Those who were sitting on them were empowered to pass judgment. I also saw the spirits of those who had been beheaded for their witness to Jesus and the word of God, those who had never worshiped the beast or its image nor accepted its mark on their foreheads or their hands. . . . The second death will have no claim on them;

they shall serve God and Christ as priests, and shall reign with
him for a thousand years [Rev. 20:4–6].

Glory belongs to those who have kept faith with Christ to the
end. They have not allowed themselves to be seduced by riches,
luxury, prostitution, or power. They have regarded all these things
as "rubbish" (Phil. 3:8). Their life has been centered on Christ.
They have clung to a higher ideal, one in which the human being is
fully realized, fully actualized. They have relativized their life, to
the point of giving it up for love of their brothers and sisters.
Whereas the generality of human beings have placed their hope in
idols, their own concern has focused on Christ and on a communion of all men and women. Steadfast in their option, not only have
they lived in this fashion, but, with the faced choice of yielding in
order to save their lives or being loyal and suffering—even suffering death—they have refused any concession whatever. No false
prudence, no sophisms, no rationalizations could sway them. The
witness of attachment to the Lord and to the freedom of the
daughters and sons of God is radical: survival is not an adequate
reason for abandoning the struggle for the upbuilding of the new
humanity. On the contrary, in this struggle suffering is redemptive:
death generates life, death becomes a wellspring of liberation for all
humankind.

The New World

This surrender, this self-bestowal, does attain its objective. Th
new world will come:

Then I saw new heavens and a new earth. The former heavens
and the former earth had passed away, and the sea was no
longer. I also saw a new Jerusalem, the holy city, coming
down out of heaven from God, beautiful as a bride prepared
to meet her husband. I heard a loud voice from the throne cry
out: "This is God's dwelling among men. He shall dwell with
them and they shall be his people and he shall be their God
who is always with them. He shall wipe every tear from their
eyes, and there shall be no more death or mourning, crying
out or pain, for the former world has passed away."

The One who sat on the throne said to me, "See, I make all things new!" Then he said, "Write these matters down, for the words are trustworthy and true!" He went on to say: "These words are already fulfilled! I am the Alpha and the Omega, the Beginning and the End. To anyone who thirsts I will give to drink without cost from the spring of life-giving water. He who wins the victory shall inherit these gifts: I will be his God and he shall be my son [Rev. 21:1-7].

The sea, the abyss, the symbol of evil, whence the beast has come, is now no longer. The Old Testament image of marriage as a symbol of the union between God and the chosen people is taken up by Saint Paul as representing the union between Christ and the church, and now the Book of Revelation does the same. There are no longer any barriers. Communion is total. We are in the very midst of the kingdom of love, freedom, justice, and peace.

"Happy are they who wash their robes so as to have free access to the tree of life and enter the city through its gates!" (Rev. 22:14). The faithful, victorious by virtue of their perseverance and their imitation of Christ, will have full dominion in this new world. They have entered by the narrow gate (Matt. 7:13), they have bathed in the blood of the Lamb. Now they deserve to share the incorruptible legacy of glory (1 Pet. 1:4).

Let him who has ears heed the Spirit's word to the churches! (Rev. 2:11).

**PRESIDENT WENCESLAU REGIONAL PENITENTIARY
MAY 1973**

Bibliographic References

Actas de los Mártires. Translated by Daniel Ruiz Bueno. Madrid: B.A.C., 1951.

Acts of the Christian Martyrs. Translated by Herbert Musurillo. Oxford Early Christian Texts. Oxford: Oxford University Press, 1972.

Bonsirven, Joseph. *El Apocalipsis de San Juan.* Madrid: Paulinas, 1966.

Cerfaux, Lucien, and Cambier, Jules. *L'Apocalypse de Saint Jean lue aux Chrétiens.* No. 17, Lectio Divina. Paris: Cerf, 1955.

Clement of Alexandria. *Stromata.* Vol. 2, The Ante-Nicene Fathers, edited by Alexander Roberts and James Donaldson. New York: Charles Scribner's Sons, 1899.

Cyprian, Thascius Caecilius. *The Exhortation to Martyrdom.* In *Actas de los Mártires.*

————. *The Lapsed.* In *Treatises,* translated by Roy J. Deferrari. Vol. 36, *The Fathers of the Church.* New York: Fathers of the Church, Inc., 1958.

————. *Letters* (1–81). Translated by Rose Bernard Donna. Vol. 51, The Fathers of the Church. Washington, D. C.: The Catholic University of America Press, 1964.

Daniélou, Jean, and Marrou, Henri. *The First Six Hundred Years.* Vol. 1, The Christian Centuries: A New History of the Catholic Church. New York: McGraw-Hill, 1964.

Eusebius Pamphili. *Ecclesiastical History.* Translated by Roy J. Deferrari. Vols. 19 and 29, The Fathers of the Church. Washington, D. C.: The Catholic University of America Press, 1953 (vol. 19), 1955 (vol. 29).

————. *The Martyrs of Palestine.* Vol. 1, The Ecclesiastical History and The Martyrs of Palestine. Translated by Hugh Jackson

Lawlor and John Ernest Leonard Oulton. London: S.P.C.K., 1954.

Féret, Henricus Maria. *The Apocalypse of Saint John.* Translated by Elizabeth Corathiel. London: Blackfriars, 1958.

Lactantius. *Of the Manner in Which the Persecutors Died.* Vol. 7, The Ante-Nicene Fathers. New York: Charles Scribner's Sons, 1899.

Lebreton, Jules, and Zeiller, Jacques. *L'Eglise Primitive.* Vol. 1, L'histoire de l'Eglise depuis les origines jusqu'à nos jours. Edited by A. Fliche and V. Martin. Paris: Bloud et Gay, 1946.

————. *De la fin du IIe. siècle à la Paix Constantinienne.* Vol. 2, L'histoire de l'Eglise.

Léon-Dufour, Xavier, et al., eds. *Vocabulaire de théologie biblique.* Paris: Cerf, 1978.

Lucian. *The Passing of Peregrinus.* The Loeb Classical Library, edited by T. E. Page, E. Capps, and W. H. D. Rouse, vol. 5 of *Lucian.* Cambridge, Mass.: Harvard University Press; London: William Heinemann, Ltd., 1936.

Origen. *Against Celsus.* Vol. 4, The Ante-Nicene Fathers. New York: The Christian Literature Company, 1890.

————. *An Exhortation to Martyrdom.* In *Origen,* translated by Rowan A. Greer. Ramsey, N. J., and Toronto: Paulist Press, 1979.

Robert, André, and Feuillet, André. *Introduction à la Bible,* vol. 2. Tournai: Desclée et Cie., 1959.

Suetonius. *The Twelve Caesars.* Translated by Robert Graves. No. L 72, The Penguin Classics. Baltimore: Penguin Books, Inc., 1957.

Tacitus. *The Annals of Imperial Rome.* Translated by Michael Grant. No. L 60, The Penguin Classics. Harmondsworth, Middlesex: Penguin Books, Ltd.; Baltimore: Penguin Books, Inc., 1956.